Hands-on Ideas

for Ministry with Young Teens

Heads-up | Easy | Low-Cost | Purposeful

Hands-on Ideas

for Ministry with Young Teens

Maryann Hakowski and Joyce Schoettler Jennings

Heads-up | Easy | Low-Cost | Purposeful

Saint Mary's Press
Winona, Minnesota
www.smp.org

Genuine recycled paper with 10% post-consumer waste.
Printed with soy-based ink.

The publishing team included Marilyn Kielbasa, development editor; Rebecca Fairbank, copy editor; Barbara Bartelson, production editor; Hollace Storkel, typesetter; Kenneth Hey, cover and logo designer; cover images, PhotoDisc Inc.; manufactured by the production services department of Saint Mary's Press.

The development consultants for the HELP (Heads-up, Easy, Low-Cost, and Purposeful) series included the following people:

Sarah Bush, Louisville, Kentucky

Jo Joy, Temple, Texas

Jeanne Fairbanks, Tipp City, Ohio

Kevin Kozlowski, New Carlisle, Ohio

Carole Goodwin, Louisville, Kentucky

Jennifer MacArthur, Saint Louis, Missouri

Joe Grant, Louisville, Kentucky

David Nissen, Cincinnati, Ohio

Maryann Hakowski, Belleville, Illinois

Ruthie Nonnenkamp, Prospect, Kentucky

The strategies in this book were created by the authors and the following contributors:

Jeanne Fairbanks

Jo Joy

Carole Goodwin

Ruthie Nonnenkamp

Joe Grant

The scriptural quotations herein are from the New Revised Standard Version of the Bible. Copyright © 1989 by the Division of Christian Education of the National Council of the Churches of Christ in the United States of America. All rights reserved.

Scriptural quotations indicated as adapted are not to be interpreted or used as official translations of the Scriptures.

"Doodle Prayers" in part C is from *Pathways to Praying with Teens,* by Maryann Hakowski (Saint Mary's Press, 1993), pages 88–89. Copyright © 1993 by Saint Mary's Press. All rights reserved.

Printed in the United States of America

Printing: 9 8 7 6 5 4 3 2

Year: 2009 08 07 06 05 04

ISBN 0-88489-573-4

Library of Congress Cataloging-in-Publication Data
Hakowski, Maryann
    Hands-on ideas for ministry with young teens / Maryann Hakowski and Joyce Schoettler Jennings.
        p. cm. — (Help)
ISBN 0-88489-573-4
        1. Church group work with teenagers. 2. Christian Education—Activity programs. 3. Catholic youth—Religious life. I. Jennings, Joyce Schoettler. II. Title. III. HELP (Series : Winona, Minn.)
BX2347.8.Y7 H25 2001
259'.23—dc21
                                                                                        00-012960

Contents

Part B: Active Learning Strategies

Part C: Prayer and Faith-Building Strategies

Introduction

Hands-on Ideas for Ministry with Young Teens is one of seven books in the HELP series—a collection of **H**eads-up, **E**asy, **L**ow-Cost, and **P**urposeful activities for young adolescents. These strategies are designed to be used as part of a comprehensive youth ministry program for grades six to eight. The strategies can stand alone or complement a religious education curriculum.

The other books in the HELP series are as follows:

- ◎ *Community-Building Ideas for Ministry with Young Teens*
- ◎ *Family Ideas for Ministry with Young Teens*
- ◎ *Holiday and Seasonal Ideas for Ministry with Young Teens*
- ◎ *Justice and Service Ideas for Ministry with Young Teens*
- ◎ *Prayer Ideas for Ministry with Young Teens*
- ◎ *Retreat Ideas for Ministry with Young Teens*

These books are helpful resources for anyone who works with young adolescents in a church or school setting. They can provide a strong foundation for a year-round, total youth ministry program whose goal is to evangelize young adolescents and support them in their faith journey.

Overview of This Book

Hands-on Ideas for Ministry with Young Teens may be used by a coordinator of youth ministry, a director of religious education, catechists, teachers, a parish youth ministry team, or any adult who works with young teens. Ownership of the book includes permission to duplicate any part of it for use with program participants.

The book's strategies are organized into three parts:

- ◎ **Part A: Reflection and Discussion Strategies** contains activities for personal reflection, self-disclosure, and affirmation.

◎ **Part B: Active Learning Strategies** includes a variety of activities for learning and reviewing factual material.
◎ **Part C: Prayer and Faith-Building Strategies** is a collection of ideas for prayer and reflection that engage young teens at many different levels.

Format of the Strategies

Each strategy begins with a brief description of its purpose. The next element is a suggested time for the activity. This is flexible and takes into account several variables, such as the size of the group, the comfort level of the participants, and whether you want to include a break. Use the suggested time as a starting point and modify it according to your circumstances. It is a good idea to include time for a break within the longer strategies.

Next is a description of the size of the group that the strategy was written for. Most of the strategies work with a range of group sizes. If your group is large, be sure to recruit enough adults to help with logistics and supervision. A good rule to follow is that for every six to eight young teens, one adult should be present.

In some strategies a section on special considerations follows the one on group size. It includes things such as notices about remote preparation requirements and cautions to pay special attention to a particular developmental issue of early adolescence.

A complete checklist of materials needed is the next part of the presentation of every strategy. A detailed description of the strategy's procedure is then provided, followed by alternative approaches. Those alternatives may be helpful in adapting the strategy to the needs of your group.

Frequently included is a list of scriptural passages that may be used with the strategy for reflection or prayer. The list is not exhaustive; a Bible concordance will provide additional citations if you want to add a more substantial scriptural component to a strategy.

The final element in each strategy offers space for keeping notes about how you might want to use the strategy in the future or change it to fit the needs of your group.

Programming Ideas

The strategies in this book can be used in a variety of ways. Consider the following suggestions:
◎ The program coordinator, catechists, teachers, and coordinator of youth ministry may collaborate to plan youth meetings and special activities that use strategies from this and other books in the HELP series.

◎ Schoolteachers may use ideas from this and other books in the HELP series to supplement their day-to-day curriculum and to add a fun dimension to classroom learning processes.

◎ Many of the strategies in the HELP series can be adapted for use with multi-generational groups.

Standard Materials

Many of the items in the materials checklists are common to several strategies in the series. To save time consider gathering frequently used materials in convenient bins and storing those bins in a place that is accessible to all staff and volunteer leaders. Some recommendations for how to organize such bins follow.

Supply Bin

The following items frequently appear in materials checklists:

◎ Bibles, at least one for every two participants
◎ masking tape
◎ cellophane tape
◎ washable and permanent markers (thick and thin)
◎ pens or pencils
◎ self-stick notes
◎ scissors
◎ newsprint
◎ blank paper, scrap paper, and notebook paper
◎ postcards
◎ notepaper
◎ envelopes
◎ baskets
◎ candles and matches
◎ items to create a prayer space (e.g., a colored cloth, a cross, a bowl of water, and a vase for flowers)

Craft Bin

Many of the strategies use craft activities to involve the young people. Consider collecting the following supplies in a separate bin:

◎ construction paper
◎ yarn and string, in assorted colors
◎ poster board
◎ glue and glue sticks
◎ fabric paints
◎ glitter and confetti

- used greeting cards
- beads
- modeling clay
- paintbrushes and paints
- crayons
- used magazines and newspapers
- hole punches
- scissors
- stickers of various kinds
- index cards
- gift wrap and ribbon

Music Bin

Young people often find deep and profound meaning in the music and lyrics of songs, both past and present. Also, the right music can set an appropriate mood for a prayer or activity. Begin with a small collection of tapes or CDs in a music bin and add to it over time. You might ask the young people to put some of their favorite music in the bin. The bin might include the following styles of music:

- *Fun gathering music that is neither current nor popular with young teens.* Ideas are well-known classics (e.g., *Overture to William Tell, Stars and Stripes Forever,* and *1812 Overture*), songs from musical theater productions, children's songs, and Christmas songs for use any time of the year.
- *Prayerful, reflective instrumental music, such as the kind that is available in the adult alternative, or New Age, section of music stores.* Labels that specialize in this type of music include Windham Hill and Narada.
- *Popular songs with powerful messages.* If you are not well versed in popular music, ask the young people to offer suggestions.
- *The music of contemporary Christian artists.* Most young teens are familiar with Amy Grant, Michael W. Smith, and Steven Curtis Chapman. Also include the work of Catholic musicians, such as David W. Kauffman, Steve Angrisano, Bruce Deaton, Sarah Hart, Jesse Manibusan, and Jessica Alles.

Other Helpful Resources

In addition to the seven books in the HELP series, the following resources can be useful in your ministry with young adolescents. All the books in the following list are published by Saint Mary's Press and can be obtained by calling or writing us at the phone number and address listed in the "Your Comments or Suggestions" section at the end of this introduction.

Catechism Connection for Teens series, by Lisa-Marie Calderone-Stewart and Ed Kunzman (1999).

That First Kiss and Other Stories

My Wish List and Other Stories

Better Than Natural and Other Stories

Straight from the Heart and Other Stories

Meeting Frankenstein and Other Stories

The five books in this collection contain short, engaging stories for teens on the joys and struggles of adolescent life, each with a reflection connecting the story to a Catholic Christian belief. Each book's faith connections reflect teachings from a different part of the *Catechism of the Catholic Church.*

The Catholic Youth Bible, edited by Brian Singer-Towns (2000). The most youth-friendly Bible for Catholic teens available. The scriptural text is accompanied by hundreds of articles to help young people pray, study, and live the Scriptures.

Faith Works for Junior High: Scripture- and Tradition-Based Sessions for Faith Formation, by Lisa-Marie Calderone-Stewart (1993). A series of twelve active meeting plans on various topics related to the Scriptures and church life.

Guided Meditations for Junior High: Good Judgment, Gifts, Obedience, Inner Blindness, by Jane E. Ayer (1997). Four guided meditations for young teens, available on audiocassette or compact disc. A leader's guide includes the script and programmatic options. Other volumes in this series, called A Quiet Place Apart, will also work with young teens.

Life Can Be a Wild Ride: More Prayers by Young Teens, edited by Marilyn Kielbasa (2001). A collection of over 230 prayers by and for young adolescents in grades six to eight.

Looking Past the Sky: Prayers by Young Teens, edited by Marilyn Kielbasa (1999). A collection of 274 prayers by and for young adolescents in grades six to eight.

One-Day Retreats for Junior High Youth, by Geri Braden-Whartenby and Joan Finn Connelly (1997). Six retreats that each fit into a school day or an afternoon or evening program. Each retreat contains a variety of icebreakers, prayers, group exercises, affirmations, and guided meditations.

Prayers with Pizzazz for Junior High Teens, by Judi Lanciotti (1996). A variety of creative prayer experiences that grab young teens' attention. The prayers are useful in many different settings, such as classes, meetings, prayer services, and retreats.

ScriptureWalk Junior High: Bible Themes, by Maryann Hakowski (1999). Eight 90-minute sessions to help bring youth and the Bible together. Each session applies biblical themes to the life issues that concern young teens.

Connections to the Discovering Program

The Discovering Program, published by Saint Mary's Press, is a religious education program for young people in grades six to eight. It consists of fourteen six-session minicourses. Each session is 1 hour long and based on the principles of active learning.

The strategies in the HELP series cover themes that are loosely connected to those explored in the Discovering Program, and can be used as part of a total youth ministry program in which the Discovering curriculum is the central catechetical component. However, no strategy in the series presumes that the participants have taken a particular course in the Discovering Program, or requires that they do so. The appendices at the end of this book list the connections between the HELP strategies and the Discovering courses.

Your Comments or Suggestions

Saint Mary's Press wants to know your reactions to the strategies in the HELP series. We are also interested in new youth ministry strategies for use with young teens. If you have a comment or suggestion, please write the series editor, Marilyn Kielbasa, at 702 Terrace Heights, Winona, MN 55987-1320; call us at our toll-free number, 800-533-8095; or e-mail the editor at *mkielbasa@smp.org*. Your ideas will help improve future editions of these books.

Part A

Reflection
and Discussion Strategies

The hands-on ideas in this section include strategies for affirming young people, helping them understand themselves and one another, and giving them tools to interact effectively with others. Some of the activities involve creating things, some are simulations, and others are simply designed to take advantage of young teens' need and desire to keep moving.

Build Your Star

A Reflection Exercise on Identity

In this reflection exercise, the young people build a unique star that represents five elements of who they are. This is a good exercise to use in conjunction with a lesson on personal giftedness or service.

Suggested Time

15 to 30 minutes

Group Size

This strategy works well with groups smaller than twenty-five people.

Special Considerations

This activity may not work with young teens on the lower end of the age spectrum. The connection between shapes and colors of triangles and personal characteristics may be difficult for some to understand.

Materials Needed

- ☼ paper plates, one for each person
- ☼ scissors, one for each person
- ☼ pens or pencils
- ☼ markers
- ☼ pastel gel pens
- ☼ glue sticks, at least one for every two people
- ☼ a variety of colored paper, metallic paper, wrapping paper, textured paper, and so forth
- ☼ a Bible

PROCEDURE

Preparation. Cut out at least one of each type of triangle from the list below. Use different colors and types of paper for the triangles. The basic triangles are these:

- ◎ equilateral: three equal sides, three equal angles
- ◎ isosceles: two equal sides, two equal angles
- ◎ scalene: all sides are unequal
- ◎ obtuse: one angle is larger than ninety degrees
- ◎ acute: all angles are less than ninety degrees
- ◎ right: one angle is ninety degrees

You can make the triangles different sizes, but in the end you should be able to create a star on a paper plate with the triangles and have the corners of the bases touching each other.

1. Give each young person a paper plate, a scissors, and a pen or pencil. Have available markers, pastel gel pens, glue sticks, and a variety of papers. Tell the young people that they are going to create a star that represents five different parts of themselves. Explain that you will lead them through a reflection about the five parts of their personality. Based on the reflection, they will design a triangle that represents each part of themselves.

2. Show the teens the triangles you cut out before the session. Discuss the characteristics of each: angle size, line length, and so forth. Also explore with the teens the character traits that a certain triangle might symbolize. For example, the equilateral triangle might represent balance in a certain area. The scalene triangle—a triangle of three unequal sides—could represent a variety of interests, and so forth.

Tell the young people that you will talk about a variety of personal characteristics, and as you mention each one, they are to decide on a color and triangle shape that represents that part of them. Lead them through the following reflection. Allow time between each section for all the participants to complete their triangle before moving on to the next section. (Note: Pastel gel pens work nicely for writing on dark paper.)

Start with your physical self. Are you short? tall? lanky? bulky? Are you athletic? a couch potato? somewhere in between? Choose a paper that represents your physical traits then cut your triangle accordingly. Write "physical" on the triangle and put it on your paper plate.

Another side of your personality is your emotions. What color represents you emotionally? What kind of triangle represents your emotions? Are your emotions up and down? Do you consider yourself even-tempered? Do people know by looking at you what you're feeling? What paper and type of triangle best shows this side of you? Cut it out, write "emotional" on it, and put it on the plate with the other one.

Your social side is another part of who you are. Think about your life with your friends and family. Is it what you want it to be? Do you have lots of friends or few? Do you spend enough time with your friends, or do you want more time with them? Do you do anything socially with your family? What color represents your social side? What shape of triangle represents it? Cut out a triangle, write "social" on it, and set it on your plate.

Think about your intellectual self. Do you feel like you are intelligent? Do you use all the brain power you have? Do you feel your brain power is working with you? Do you see yourself as low on the intelligence scale? What color and what type of triangle represents this side of you? Cut it out, write "intelligence" on it, and set it on the plate with the others.

The last side of your personality is your spiritual side. Spirituality includes your values, dreams, hopes, questions about life, and your relationship with God. What color will you choose for this side? And what kind of triangle represents your spirituality? Cut it out, write "spiritual" on it, and put it with your other triangles.

3. Note that each person now has a paper plate and five triangles. Explain that they are to create a star by gluing their triangles onto the plate. The only rule is that each triangle must connect at its base to another triangle. The young teens should each write their name in the middle of the star.

Allow time for them to finish the task and compare results. You may want to display the stars in the meeting space for a while for everyone to observe and enjoy.

4. Make the following points in your own words:

You are a star in God's eyes. The star you created represents the kind of star you think you are. Each person is unique. Who you are today is not the same person you are likely to be tomorrow. We are always changing, evolving, growing into the wonderful person God intended for us to become. Our job as stars is to let our light shine for all to see.

Conclude the activity by reading Matt. 5:14–16.

ALTERNATIVE APPROACHES

- ◎ If you are using this activity with young teens who are unfamiliar with triangle types and characteristics, do not confuse them by introducing geometric language. Simply cut out the triangles in different shapes and describe them without naming them.
- ◎ If you think the young people would be willing to do so, invite them to share their stars and tell others in the group why they chose the colors and shapes of triangles that they did. This alternative requires a high degree of trust among group members.
- ◎ You may want to create a sample star so that you can demonstrate how the triangles should fit together.

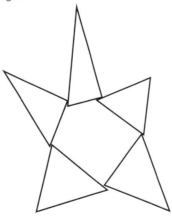

- ◎ Use small paper plates, poke a hole in the top of each, string a piece of yarn through, and use the stars to decorate a holiday tree in the meeting space.
- ◎ Create a banner of the scriptural text "You are the light of the world" (Matt. 5:14) or "Let your light shine" (Matt. 5:16) to decorate your meeting space. Attach the stars to the banner.

NOTES

Use the space below to jot notes and reminders for the next time you use this strategy.

Life in a Bag
An Introduction Activity

This self-disclosure exercise invites the young people to introduce themselves to one another using objects and symbols that represent them. It is a good activity for the beginning of a year or for a retreat.

Suggested Time

This activity takes place over two or more sessions. It will take 30 to 45 minutes to decorate the bags and 2 to 5 minutes for each person to present the contents of his or her bag at a subsequent session.

Group Size

This strategy can be done with any size group. However, if the group is larger than ten people, consider having a few people present their bag each week until everyone has had an opportunity to introduce themselves.

Materials Needed

- ☼ a paper grocery bag for each person
- ☼ craft items such as scissors, glue, markers, paints, crayons, string, yarn, old magazines and newspapers, stickers, lettering, and so forth
- ☼ a Bible

PROCEDURE

Preparation. Create your own "life in a bag" by decorating the outside of a grocery bag with your name and other basic facts about yourself. Use words, pictures, lettering, small objects, and anything else that will let the viewer see who you are.

Put several items inside the bag that identify you, such as a family picture, items that represent important events or hobbies, or things that reveal your personality.

1. Give a paper grocery bag to each young person and make craft supplies available. Display the bag you created before the session to give the teens an idea of what you are looking for. Do not show them the contents of the bag at this time.

Explain that they are to decorate their grocery bag in a way that will show other people a little about who they are. Allow about 30 minutes for the decorating process. Keep close track of time; an activity such as this one can go on for a long time if allowed to.

2. When everyone has decorated a bag, introduce yourself by unpacking the contents of your own bag. Show each item and explain its connection to your life. You may want to pass some objects around the group.

Tell the young people to take their own bag home and fill it with things that will help others get to know them. They can also continue decorating their bag if they want to do so. They should not show others what is in their bag until it is their turn to introduce themselves.

3. At the next gathering, ask for volunteers to unpack their bag and introduce themselves to others. Allow no more than 5 minutes per person.

4. Close each introduction segment by reading Ps. 138:1–3,8 and giving special thanks by name for the people that shared part of themselves with the group.

ALTERNATIVE APPROACHES

◎ This activity can be done in one session or on a retreat by asking the young people to cut out pictures from magazines and newspapers that represent them and place them in the bag. If you choose this option, use lunch bags instead of grocery bags.

◎ If the young people already know one another, have them draw names and create a "life in a bag" for someone else. They should put items in the bag that describe or symbolize what they already know about the person.

◎ Post the bags and use them as collectors for affirmation notes, secret pal exchanges, or small gifts.

NOTES

Use the space below to jot notes and reminders for the next time you use this strategy.

Being Michelangelo
An Exercise in Perspectives

This upside-down painting activity teaches perseverance, patience, tolerance, and appreciation for other people's perspectives and talents.

Suggested Time

30 to 45 minutes

Group Size

This strategy works best with twenty-five or fewer participants.

Materials Needed

- ☼ a book containing photographs of the ceiling of the Sistine Chapel and a brief biography of Michelangelo
- ☼ 11-by-17-inch paper, one sheet for each person
- ☼ masking tape
- ☼ crayons or markers
- ☼ tables or desks
- ☼ a Bible

PROCEDURE

Preparation. Prepare a short summary of the life and works of Michelangelo.

1. Display the photographs of the ceiling of the Sistine Chapel, with Michelangelo's depiction of the creation of Adam and Eve. Briefly introduce Michelangelo as a Renaissance artist and tell the young teens a little about his life and his art. While you are talking, you may want to show the young people pictures of other works that may be familiar to them, such as the Pietà or the statue of David. Be sure to tell the young people how Michelangelo painted most of the Sistine Chapel ceiling while lying on his back.

2. Explain to the young people that to gain perspective on Michelangelo's unique talents, patience, endurance, and perseverance, they are going to attempt to create as he did.

Give each person a sheet of paper, four pieces of masking tape, and a variety of markers or crayons. Direct them to lie on the floor and tape the paper under a desk or a table. Explain the following rules:

The task is to create a piece of art from the same position that Michelangelo did, that is, while lying on your back.

The artwork should contain as much detail as possible.

The entire paper must be filled with color. If you draw a figure or an object, you should also color in the background.

Allow 15 to 20 minutes for this task, depending on the young people's energy and enthusiasm.

3. After time is up, invite the young people to remove the paper from the desk or table and share it with the rest of the group.

4. Lead the group in a discussion around the following questions:

What have you learned about Michelangelo that you can apply to your own life?

As an artist Michelangelo went above and beyond the ordinary. Have you ever had to go above and beyond the ordinary? Explain what you did and the feelings you experienced.

Who in your life has a talent that you do not possess? What is your attitude toward that person's gift?

What talent do you have that is unique? How do you feel about this gift? How do other people show appreciation for it?

5. Conclude the activity with a prayer of praise to God for everyone's talents. It takes many people with many different talents to make a difference in our world. Close by reading Psalm 150.

ALTERNATIVE APPROACHES

 Instead of individual pieces of paper, tape a strip of butcher paper underneath each table. Assign as many young people to work under one table as can fit comfortably. Have them create a mural on a biblical theme, such as creation or the journey through the desert.

This activity is especially effective—albeit considerably messier—if you use real paint. Use tempera paints, but be sure to have soapy water and a sponge handy.

If painting under tables or desks is not possible, have the young people create their artwork using the hand opposite their preferred hand.

NOTES

Use the space below to jot notes and reminders for the next time you use this strategy.

Pass the Bag
A Biblical Affirmation Exercise

Most young teens love to hear good things about themselves, but many rarely get that chance. This affirmation exercise familiarizes them with scriptural values, increases their vocabulary, and builds their self-esteem.

Suggested Time

45 to 60 minutes

Group Size

This activity works best with groups of ten to twenty-five people.

Materials Needed

- ☼ Bibles, one for each person
- ☼ newsprint and markers
- ☼ masking tape
- ☼ paper lunch bags or plain popcorn bags, one for each person
- ☼ pens or pencils

☼ 2-by-4-inch pieces of paper, enough so that every person in the group has one paper for each person in the group including themselves

☼ 4-by-6-inch index cards, one for each person

PROCEDURE

Preparation. Write the following scriptural citations on newsprint and post it in the meeting space.

◎ Matt. 5:1–10
◎ Rom. 12:9–21
◎ 1 Cor. 12:4–11
◎ 1 Cor. 13:3–13
◎ Gal. 5:22–26
◎ Eph. 4:25–32

In each paper bag, put the number of small pieces of paper equal to the number of participants in the group; that is, if you have twenty people in your group, put twenty pieces of paper in each bag.

1. Form the participants into six small groups or pairs. You may want to consult another volume in the HELP series, *Community-Building Ideas for Ministry with Young Teens,* for creative ideas for forming small groups.

Give each person a Bible and each group a sheet of newsprint and some markers. Assign to each group one of the passages listed on the newsprint that you prepared before the session. Tell them to look up the passage and make a list of the positive qualities of a follower of Christ. They may need to think hard about what quality a passage is referring to. For example, "Do not let the sun go down on your anger" (Eph. 4:26) means that a follower of Christ is forgiving, reconciling, and does not hold a grudge.

Allow about 10 minutes for the groups to list the Christian qualities from their assigned passage on newsprint. Some groups may need help from you or another adult.

2. As the groups finish the task, give them some masking tape and have them post their newsprint on a wall so that everyone can see the lists. Gather the young people in a central location. Review each list and point out the variety of positive qualities that a follower of Christ possesses. Be sure that the following qualities are on the lists:

◎ loyal	◎ just	◎ truthful	◎ prudent
◎ honorable	◎ faithful	◎ joyful	◎ wise
◎ dependable	◎ loving	◎ compassionate	◎ forgiving
◎ responsible	◎ kind	◎ generous	◎ patient
◎ hopeful	◎ helpful	◎ fair	◎ gentle
◎ courageous	◎ respectful	◎ honest	

3. Give each person a bag and a pen or pencil. Pass around some markers and tell the young people to write their name on their bag. Call their attention to the slips of paper in their bag. Explain the following directions in your own words:

Take one slip of paper from your bag. Choose three words from the lists on the wall that describe your character strengths and write them on the paper. Put a star on your paper, fold it, and put it back in the bag.

When I give you a signal, pass the bag to your left. Look at the name on the bag you receive, pull out a slip of paper, choose three qualities from the list that describe that person, and write them on the slip. Think carefully about the person whose bag you have. Do not be afraid to ask the Holy Spirit for guidance in choosing the best words for that person. Do not put a star on this or any other slip, but fold it and put it back in the bag.

Follow the same procedure for every bag that comes to you until you get your own bag back.

4. When the bags have returned to their owners, give the young people time to read the contents of their bag. They might want to tally the characteristics and compare them with the ones they wrote about themselves in the first part of the exercise.

5. While the young people are reading their notes, distribute one 4-by-6-inch index card to each person. When they are finished reading, ask them to complete the following sentence-starters on the index card. They should not write their name on the card.

◎ Something I liked about this activity is . . .
◎ Something I didn't like about this exercise is . . .
◎ The quality others see in me that surprised me is . . .
◎ A quality I would like to develop more in myself is . . .

6. Collect the cards. Encourage the young people to take their bag home to remind themselves of the good qualities other people see in them.
    Close by reading 1 Thess. 5:13b–23.

ALTERNATIVE APPROACHES

- Some young people may be conscious of others identifying their handwriting. If this is true in your group, suggest that they print or write with the hand they do not usually write with.
- Personalize the closing scriptural passage by inserting a name or names of people in your group between exhortations. For example:
  - Be at peace among yourselves, Rashid and Bryan. And we urge you, Vanessa, Haley, and Jana, to admonish the idlers, encourage the faint-hearted, help the weak, be patient with all of them. Jerome, Tiffany, and B.J., see that none of you repays evil for evil . . ." (adapted from 1 Thess. 5:13b–15).

NOTES

Use the space below to jot notes and reminders for the next time you use this strategy.

Wander and Ponder

A Reflection and Dialogue Activity

OVERVIEW

This activity invites the young people to spend quiet time pondering life's questions and then dialogue with another person about them. While doing so, they move from place to place, as Jesus moved from city to city on his journeys, teaching people how to find answers to those questions. This is an ideal activity for a retreat or youth gathering.

Suggested Time

45 to 60 minutes

Group Size

This activity works with any size group as long as adequate supervision is available.

Materials Needed

No special materials are required.

PROCEDURE

Preparation. Plan a route for the group that will take them away from the building and back in the time you have available for this activity.

1. Announce that the object of the next block of time is to "wander and ponder." Mention that Jesus walked from place to place during his ministry. Sometimes he walked alone, like when he went off by himself to pray. At other times he had conversations with people, as he did on the road to Emmaus.

Explain that you will present the participants with a question or two at the beginning of the walk. After that you will simply be the timekeeper, making sure that each part of the process is given about one quarter of the time available. Outline the following process in your own words:

During the first quarter of the walk, think silently about the question. Do not talk to anyone else.

When I call time, pair up with someone and talk about the question. Challenge each other to go deeper into the question and see different perspectives. Ask your partner questions such as, "Why do you think that?" or "What experience in your life makes you believe those things?" Share life experiences and faith stories from your own life, but make sure your partner gets a chance to share also.

At the third signal, wander silently again and ponder the conversation between you and your partner. What does it mean to you? How does it help your faith? Do you need to change? If so, how?

At the fourth signal, walk and talk to your partner about anything related or not related to the original question. At this point we will return to our meeting place.

2. Present one or two of the following questions to the group, or make up your own questions to correlate this activity with your current lesson, theme, or liturgical season. Suggest that they repeat the question a number of times to themselves as they begin their walk. This will help them get into a reflection mode.

What does God look like?

What question would you like to ask God?

Why is God and church so important to so many people?

What happens after death?

Is there life after death?

Where is heaven, and what is it like?

Where is hell, and what is it like?

Follow the process outlined above, keeping track of time so that each part is given equal time.

3. When you return to the starting place, present one or more of the following evaluative questions to the group.

What did you like about this experience?

What didn't you like?

Share one thought you had.

Share one thought you heard from your partner.

ALTERNATIVE APPROACHES

◎ If you have time before the walk, explore the Gospels with the group for examples of times when Jesus wandered and pondered, either alone or with others.

◎ To avoid the natural pairing of friends and the emotional trauma of those who do not fit in to a group, you may want to assign partners before the walk begins.

◎ If you have an extended period of time, choose several questions. For each question allow for individual reflection time and dialogue with a partner. Stop in between each question to give people a chance to rest, have a snack, discuss the question as a group, and get ready for the next question.

◎ Have the young people ponder scriptural passages and related questions. Possibilities include Luke 12:22–34, John 3:1–21, or the lectionary readings from the past or upcoming week.

NOTES

Use the space below to jot notes and reminders for the next time you use this strategy.

You Can Do It!

A Learning Activity on Endurance

OVERVIEW   This exercise will help the young teens reflect on the meaning of endurance and think about the place of this virtue in the life of a follower of Jesus.

Suggested Time

30 to 45 minutes

Group Size

This strategy works with any size group.

Materials Needed

- ☼ newsprint and markers
- ☼ a bag of treats, such as candies, wrapped cookies, small toys, or coins
- ☼ a Bible for each person

PROCEDURE

Preparation. List the following scriptural citations on newsprint:

- Ex. 14:1–31
- Matt. 4:1–11
- Acts 11:19–26
- 1 Thess. 3:6–13
- 1 Pet. 3:13–18

1. Create small teams of no fewer than three people but no more than six. Another volume in the HELP series, *Community-Building Ideas for Ministry with Young Teens,* includes creative ideas for forming small groups.

Explain that you will give the teams a series of exercises to do. Besides each person doing the task themselves, they should support other team members, encouraging them to stay with the task as long as possible.

2. Lead the teams through the following series of exercises. Present the winning team of each exercise with the treat bag and allow team members to choose a prize.

Stand on one leg without holding on to anyone or anything. When a person puts his or her free leg down or falls over, that person is out. The team with the last person standing on one leg wins.

Hold your arms straight out to the side without supporting them on anyone or anything. A person is out when one or both arms drop below his or her shoulder blades. The team with the last person standing with arms extended wins.

Kneel on the floor with your back straight and with no support from anyone or anything. Hold your arms straight up in the air. A person is out when her or his arms move down past her or his ears. The last person left with arms straight up wins for her or his team.

3. Lead the group in a discussion of the following questions:

Which activity was the easiest for you? the hardest? Why?

What one word describes what you were expected to do? [Accept all possible answers, then introduce the word *endurance.*]

Besides today, name some other times when you practice endurance.

How does endurance relate to being a Christian?

4. Display the list of scriptural citations that you created before the session. Assign one passage to each team. If you have more teams than citations, assign the same passage to more than one team. They are to read the passage and figure out what it has to say about endurance. Allow about 5 minutes for the teams to read and discuss the passage.

Invite a spokesperson from each team to share the passage with the rest of the group and explain what their team decided its message about endurance was.

5. Close the session by encouraging the young people to look for other people in their life who possess a strong sense of endurance, particularly in life's difficult and challenging times.

ALTERNATIVE APPROACHES

◎ Instead of doing the endurance activities in teams, do them as a large group. Add more activities or replace the ones in this plan with something that seems more appropriate for your group.

◎ Close the activity with a prayer service during which the young people pray silently or aloud for situations in their life where they need the virtue of endurance. Use one or more of the readings from the newsprint list for the prayer.

NOTES

Use the space below to jot notes and reminders for the next time you use this strategy.

Soaring Spirits
An Affirmation Project

OVERVIEW

In this craft project, the young teens build and fly kites, affirming themselves and others in the process. This activity is definitely designed to make their spirits soar. It is a wonderful choice for a retreat or an extended meeting during kite-flying months.

Suggested Time

Approximately 60 minutes to build the kites and do the affirmation process. Allow extra time if the weather is conducive to kite flying.

Group Size

This activity can be done with any size group. If you have more than fifteen participants, other adults will need to help with the craft project and lead small groups during the affirmation part of the activity.

Materials Needed

- a kite-making kit for each person
- extra paper for kite tails if not included in kit
- crayons or markers
- masking tape
- string for flying the kites
- a Bible

PROCEDURE

Preparation. Purchase kite-making kits from a local craft or hobby store. Make sure the kites are plain white without any design or decoration. If kite tails are not included in the kits, have extra paper available for adding kite tails. Assemble one of the kites prior to your meeting so you have an example to show the young teens and are better able to explain the directions.

1. Introduce this activity by making the following points in your own words:

Everyone needs to learn how to look for the good inside themselves before they can recognize the good in others.

We will make something today that will help everyone's spirit soar. We are going to learn more about ourselves and one another and then give our good words a chance to take flight.

2. Distribute the kite-making kits and explain the directions for assembling the kites. Display the model that you created before the session. Allow enough time for everyone to finish assembling their kite before giving the next direction.

3. Make crayons and markers available to the group. Direct the teens to write their first name in the center of their kite. Invite them to write words or draw pictures on the kite that describe good qualities about themselves. They should aim for at least five, but allow them to add more. Urge them to focus on gifts and talents rather than physical, superficial features such as "nice clothes." You may want to share the examples you wrote on your sample kite.

4. When the young people have finished their kites, hang them up around the room. Invite the teens to walk around and add affirmations to one another's kite tails. If they have been together in small groups for this activity, ask them to write something for everyone in their group first. Remind the young people that their comments must be positive gifts and talents that they see in one another.

5. If weather permits, allow some time to go outside and fly the kites. You may want to display the kites in your meeting space for a few weeks. Then allow the young people to take them home and hang them in their room as a reminder of the good qualities they recognize in themselves and the good qualities and gifts others see in them. Encourage them to continue affirming and building up one another.

6. Close the activity with a prayer thanking God for the gifts we have and the gifts we see in others. Use one of the scriptural passages below.

ALTERNATIVE APPROACHES

◉ If you are working with a small group of teens, you may want to make one large kite to display on the wall of your meeting space instead of individual smaller kites. By doing this the teens will have a clear picture of the total giftedness of the group. Include yourself in the process of naming gifts.

◉ This is an ideal activity for young teens to do with younger children during a camp or vacation Bible school. The teens can help the children put together the kites, decorate them, and fly them.

SCRIPTURAL CONNECTIONS

◉ Isa. 40:28–31
◉ Eph. 1:15–19
◉ Phil. 2:1–4

NOTES

Use the space below to jot notes and reminders for the next time you use this strategy.

The Light of Christ
A Candleholder-Making Activity

This activity celebrates the role of light in our life. The light in our Catholic faith is Jesus, the light of the world. The young teens have an opportunity to make a prayer candleholder as a symbol of the light of Jesus shining in their lives, and as a reminder of his call to be lights for the world.

Suggested Time

30 to 45 minutes

Group Size

This craft project can be done with any size group. Additional adult help is needed for larger groups.

Special Considerations

The candleholders will need to dry completely before a candle can be burned inside them. This may take 30 minutes or more. You may want to make the holders at the beginning of your session and use them for prayer at the end of your session. Another option is to make the holders one day and use them for prayer another day.

Materials Needed

- ☼ used newspapers
- ☼ empty baby food jars, one for each person
- ☼ paper plates, one for each person
- ☼ white glue in disposable bowls
- ☼ paintbrushes, no larger than 1 inch, one for every two or three people
- ☼ scissors, one for each person
- ☼ a variety of brightly colored tissue paper
- ☼ clear shellac or decoupage covering, such as Mod Podge
- ☼ votive candles, one for each person
- ☼ matches

PROCEDURE

Preparation. You may want to cover the tables with newspaper so the shellac does not damage the tables. Doing so also makes cleanup much easier.

Soak the baby food jars in water to remove the labels. Make a sample candleholder, following the directions given in the procedure steps.

1. Announce to the young people that they will make their own candleholder in this activity. Introduce the activity by making the following comments in your own words:

When we gather for special events, light is often an important part of the celebration. We light candles on a birthday cake, put lights on a Christmas tree, light sparklers on the Fourth of July, and so forth.

When Christians gather to celebrate, light is also part of the celebration. A candle flame is a reminder of the presence of God in our life. We are reminded that Jesus is the light of our world, and that he calls us to be light for one another.

2. Give each young person a baby food jar and a paper plate. Make bowls of glue, paintbrushes, scissors, and tissue paper available. Explain the following directions in your own words:

Decide which colors of paper you want to use for your candleholder. You will need at least two colors, but you can use as many as you want. Cut the paper into small squares of no larger than one-half inch.

Put your jar upside down on a paper plate to prevent it from sticking to the newspaper on the table. Use a paintbrush to cover the bottom and outside surface of the baby food jar with a thin layer of glue. You may want to cover a small part of the jar at one time so that the glue does not dry before you put the paper on.

Arrange the squares of paper on the jar, overlapping them slightly to create a stained-glass effect. Do not glue paper inside the jar or on the rim.

When the jar is covered with paper, paint a thin coat of clear shellac or Mod Podge over the surface. Allow it to dry.

3. Give everyone a votive candle to place inside their jar. Use the candles as part of a prayer service on the theme of being lights in the world or in a seasonal service, such as during Advent or Lent.

ALTERNATIVE APPROACHES

- If your group is small, you may make one large candleholder. Use a larger jar and a small pillar candle instead of a votive candle. Let the candle become the group's prayer candle.
- To save time, you may want to cut the paper into squares before the session and put them in small bowls. Place the bowls where everyone can have access to them.

SCRIPTURAL CONNECTIONS

- Matt. 5:14–16 (You are the light of the world.)
- John 1:1–9 (Jesus, the light in our darkness)
- John 8:12 (Jesus tells us that he is the light of the world.)

NOTES

Use the space below to jot notes and reminders for the next time you use this strategy.

Excuses, Excuses
A Drama and Discussion Activity

This activity uses drama to begin a discussion on the many excuses people make for not going to liturgy. It encourages the young teens to make time for God and to make the celebration of the Eucharist a priority in their life.

Suggested Time

About 30 to 45 minutes for the introduction, preparation, and follow-up discussion. The actual time will depend on how many small groups you have presenting their skits.

Group Size

This activity works best with groups of thirty or fewer people arranged in small groups of four or five people each.

Materials Needed

- ☼ newsprint and markers
- ☼ a variety of props, hats, and other clothing items (optional)

PROCEDURE

1. Ask the young people what kinds of things keep them busy or how they spend their time. List their answers on newsprint.

After you have filled a page, ask how much time they spend paying attention to God. Some teens may spend a few minutes every day in prayer. Others may say that they only pay attention to God when they go to church on Sunday.

2. Make the following comments in your own words:

Getting to know God—like developing any friendship—takes time. Just as we spend time with our friends, we need to make time for God. One place to start is by making sure we celebrate the Eucharist with our parish community every week.

People of all ages make excuses for not going to Mass. For a teenager it might be because he or she had a hard week and needs to catch up on sleep. For a family it may be because someone has to play in a soccer game or march in a parade. Everyone has probably used an excuse not to go to Mass, or at least thought of one.

3. Invite the young people to call out some of the excuses that they have heard. List their ideas on newsprint. After you have listed at least ten excuses, form the young people into groups of four or five. You may want to consult another volume in the HELP series, *Community-Building Ideas for Ministry with Young Teens,* for creative suggestions for forming small groups.

Invite each group to choose one of the excuses and create a skit about the situation. The skit should be 1 to 2 minutes long and should involve everyone in the group. If you have props, hats, or other articles of clothing, make them available to the young people.

4. Allow about 10 minutes for the teens to plan their skit before giving them this further instruction: They will have to present their skit twice: once as they have just planned, and a second time with an additional character—Jesus. Allow about 5 minutes for them to make adjustments for the additional character.

5. Invite the groups to present their skits, first without and then with Jesus as a character. After all the skits have been presented, lead a discussion around the following questions:

How did your group decide which excuse to create a skit about?

How did the skit change when you found out that Jesus would be an additional character in the second presentation of the skit?

What did you learn from this activity?

6. Announce that together you will create a new list. This time you want them to call out reasons to go to the weekly liturgy. List all their reasons on newsprint. Try to get at least ten on the list.

ALTERNATIVE APPROACHES

◎ Ask the teens to compose a letter from Jesus to us, inviting us to come to Mass. What do they think Jesus would say? Why do they think Jesus wants them to come and spend some time with him?

◎ If you have time, form the young people into small groups first. Have each group create a newsprint list of excuses. Compare the lists and tell each group to choose one excuse for their group skit. Do the same with the list of reasons to go to Mass.

◎ Get permission for the teens to present their skits at a parish function where adults will be present.

◎ Use the same idea, but instead of coming up with excuses for not going to Mass, list the excuses for not volunteering for the variety of tasks that are part of parish life, such as teaching in the formation program or singing in the choir. Get permission for the teens to present their skits at Sunday liturgies prior to commitment Sunday at the beginning of the year.

◎ Before the next meeting, make up a card with ten excuses for not going to Mass and ten reasons that we should go. Use a standard sign such as a red circle with a line through it on the list of excuses. Make a copy for each person and distribute them at the next session. You might also make them available to the whole parish.

SCRIPTURAL CONNECTIONS

◎ Matt. 26:26–30 (The Last Supper)
◎ Luke 22:14–20 (The Last Supper)
◎ Luke 24:28–35 (The walk to Emmaus)
◎ Acts 2:43–47 (Life in the early church)

NOTES

Use the space below to jot notes and reminders for the next time you use this strategy.

Feelings Charades
A Communication Activity

This drama activity highlights nonverbal communication, especially in how people share feelings with one another. It also stresses that feelings in themselves are not good or bad; it is what we do with them and how we act on them that can be positive or negative.

Suggested Time

30 to 40 minutes

Group Size

This activity works best with groups of up to fifty teens. If your group is larger than ten people, you will need to form the participants into smaller groups.

Materials Needed

- ☼ newsprint and markers
- ☼ 3-by-5-inch index cards, about thirty, cut in half to be 3-by-2½ inches
- ☼ pens or pencils

PROCEDURE

1. Introduce the session by noting that it is usually a lot easier to give someone directions ("Go around the corner to the second door on the left") or tell someone a fact ("My dad and I cleaned out the garage yesterday") than it is to share feelings ("I feel angry when you poke fun at my clothes"). Yet communicating feelings is one of the most important things we can do in our relationships.

Invite the teens to call out as many feelings as they can think of. Write down their suggestions on newsprint until you have forty to fifty feelings listed.

2. Arrange the participants in small groups of six to ten people. Give each small group fifteen small index cards and pens or pencils. Tell them to choose fifteen feeling words from the newsprint, write each word on a separate card, and place the cards in a pile, facedown.

After all the groups are finished, appoint someone from each group to swap cards with another group and, without looking at the new cards, place them facedown in the center of their group.

3. Explain that in turn, each person in the group should take a card and read it to themselves without anyone else seeing it. Without speaking, using only facial expressions and body language, the person is to communicate that feeling to the group. The other group members must guess the feeling being portrayed. You may want to set a time limit of 1 minute or so for the group to guess the feeling.

Each person in the group should have at least one turn. Go around twice if time permits.

4. Gather all the groups together and lead a discussion around the following questions:

How hard was it to convey feelings without using words?

What are some other ways people convey feelings?

Which feelings are easiest to express in words? Which are hardest?

What did you learn about communication from this exercise?

5. Close by stressing the importance of communicating our feelings to others and being aware of the ways others communicate their feelings to us.

ALTERNATIVE APPROACHES

◎ If additional time is available, include time to practice verbal communication of feelings. The most common exercises involve "I messages," such as "I feel _____ when _____." Invite the young people to practice sharing "I messages" in role-plays of different situations they might encounter at home or in school.

Several types of posters with feeling words and facial expressions are available. Use such a poster to gauge the feelings in the group periodically. One such poster is available through Free Spirit Publishing, 217 Fifth Avenue North, Minneapolis, MN 55401-1299; 800-735-7323; Web site *www.freespirit.com*.

NOTES

Use the space below to jot notes and reminders for the next time you use this strategy.

If I Were Candy
A Self-Disclosure Activity

This low-level self-disclosure activity is an edible icebreaker designed to get the young people to use their imagination to describe themselves and begin the process of sharing. It is best used as an opening activity for a meeting or session. It can also be used effectively within a retreat.

Suggested Time

Allow about 5 minutes for the young people to choose a kind of candy and then about 1 minute per person to share how the candy describes themselves.

Group Size

If you have fewer than twenty young people, you can do this with the entire group. If your group is larger, form smaller groups of eight to ten people each.

Special Considerations

Some younger teens, depending on their level of cognitive maturity, may have a difficult time relating something like candy to their personality. If your group consists of young people who fall at the young end of the spectrum, you may need to give extra examples and more explicit directions.

Materials Needed

☼ assorted candy items, about ten more than the number of people in your group

PROCEDURE

1. Spread all the candy in the center of a table so that all items are clearly visible. Do not allow anyone to take an item until you are finished giving all the directions for the activity.

2. Ask the young people to take a candy that best describes themselves. They will need to talk about why they chose the item, so encourage them to think about it first. They should avoid grabbing the candy nearest to them or their favorite candy. In fact, the candy that symbolizes them the most may be one that they do not even like! Provide the following examples:

I chose the M&Ms because they are different colors on the outside, and I like to do a lot of different things, like play the trumpet, play soccer, belong to scouts, watch movies. They are also soft and sweet on the inside, and I really try to be sweet to others.

I chose a PayDay candy bar because sometimes I feel pulled in all sorts of directions like the inside of the bar. But I can also have fun and be kind of nutty, like the nuts on the outside of the candy bar.

I chose the caramels because what you see is what you get! I also last a long time and can stick to a job until it is finished. And I'm good at sticking by my friends.

Tell them that they can make the same choice as someone else because their explanation will likely be different.

3. When everyone has taken a candy item, allow time for each person in turn to explain how the choice describes him or her.

4. When everyone has shared, lead the group in a discussion around the following questions:

How is candy like people?

Which candy would you choose to represent God?

What did you learn from this activity?

Encourage the teens to recognize and celebrate the uniqueness and the goodness of each person. Then celebrate by eating the candy!

SCRIPTURAL CONNECTIONS

- ◎ Gen. 1:26–31 (God created human beings.)
- ◎ Psalm 139 (Marvelous are God's works!)
- ◎ Luke 1:46–55 (My soul magnifies the Lord.)
- ◎ Rom. 12:1–8 (We have many gifts but the same Spirit.)

ALTERNATIVE APPROACHES

- ◎ At the end of the exercise, invite the young people to choose a candy item that describes their group or each person in their family.
- ◎ If the teens in your group know one another fairly well, use this as an affirmation exercise. Assign each person someone else in the group and ask them to choose a candy that represents that person. Emphasize that the reasons for choosing the particular type of candy should be complimentary.

NOTES

Use the space below to jot notes and reminders for the next time you use this strategy.

In Sync

A Lesson in Group Dynamics

This activity challenges the young people to recognize how every new person changes the dynamic of a group and how we must adapt to this change in order to make everyone feel welcome and part of the group. It is a good activity to use on a retreat or when someone new joins an established group.

Suggested Time

15 to 20 minutes

Group Size

This activity works best with a minimum of eight people.

Materials Needed

☼ Nerf-type balls, one for every eight to ten participants

PROCEDURE

1. If your group is larger than fifteen people, create smaller groups of eight to ten. Give each group a Nerf ball and ask them to stand in a circle.

Tell the person holding the ball to state his or her name and then pass the ball to another person in the group who has not had the ball. Continue until everyone has had a turn. The only rule is that they cannot pass the ball to the person on either side of them. The last person to get the ball throws it back to the first person. The pattern the group establishes in the first round must be repeated each time.

Give the participants time to practice the pattern in their group until it is smooth.

2. Take one person out of each group and switch him or her with someone in another group. Each group then has one new person. Tell the teens to continue playing the game. Observe what they do when a new person is added. Do not give any instructions or directives. If they ask, simply tell them that they need to figure it out.

Once things are running smoothly, switch two people from each group. Once again observe what happens.

3. Gather the participants and lead them in a discussion around the following questions:

What was it like when people were switched in and out of the group?

If you were one of the people who was switched, how did it feel when you were taken out of one group and inserted into another?

What did you learn about communication from this activity?

What did you learn about adding new people to a group?

How can you take what you learned and put it into action?

ALTERNATIVE APPROACHES

◎ If you have a small group, leave a few people outside the circle the first time you play this game. For each successive round, add one or more people to the circle. Add these questions to your discussion:
  ◎ What did it feel like to be on the inside of the circle while others were left out?
  ◎ What did it feel like to be on the outside?
  This alternative would work even if you have a large group. Leave three or four people out of every circle. Add them to the circles at the appropriate intervals.

◎ To make things more complex, give each group two or three balls or objects to juggle in a pattern.

- Tell the participants to state their own name and the name of the person they are throwing the ball to. This directive will make it slightly more difficult for the new people who are added to the circle.
- Follow this activity with a discussion about cliques and welcoming everyone into one's circle of friends.

SCRIPTURAL CONNECTIONS

- Rom. 8:28
- Rom. 12:1–8
- 2 Thess. 3:6–13

NOTES

Use the space below to jot notes and reminders for the next time you use this strategy.

Here I Am!

A Self-Disclosure and Affirmation Activity

In this strategy the young teens create a life-size body poster on which they write positive qualities about themselves and one another. In the process they acknowledge their own gifts and affirm the gifts of others. This activity works well on a retreat or in an extended session as part of a lesson on using one's talents for the Reign of God.

Suggested Time

About 40 minutes, depending on the number of young people in your group

Group Size

This strategy works with any size group, as long as enough adults are available to supervise the activity.

Special Considerations

You will need a large open area for the young people to work in, such as a gym or a cafeteria. The area should be large enough to accommodate a 6- to 7-foot-long piece of newsprint or butcher paper for each person. You will also need adequate wall space to hang the pieces when they are finished.

Materials Needed

- a roll of newsprint or butcher paper
- scissors
- markers
- masking tape
- a Bible

PROCEDURE

Preparation. Cut a sheet of newsprint or butcher paper 6 to 7 feet long for each person. The young teens will have to lay on the paper and have someone trace their body, so be sure to have a few sheets of paper that are about a foot longer than the tallest person in the group.

You may want to create a poster of yourself as a model of the activity and the types of things you are looking for.

1. Assign each person a partner. You may want to consult another volume in the HELP series, *Community-Building Ideas for Ministry with Young Teens,* for creative ideas for forming pairs. Depending on the comfort level of the teens, you may want to have people of the same gender working together for the first part of the activity.

2. Give each person a sheet of paper that you cut before the session and several markers. Tell them to write the words "Here I am!" at the top of the page and their name in large letters. Then they are to take turns lying on the paper while their partner traces the outline of their body.

3. Ask the young people to close their eyes or look at their silhouette and remain quiet while you introduce the activity. Then lead them through a short reflection by making the following points in your own words:

Pretend you are looking in the mirror. What do you see? Hair that's a little out of place? A funny face? A smile? . . . What else do you see? . . . Look a little harder in the mirror. . . . Look beyond what is on the outside. . . . What kind of person are you? . . . What do you have to offer the world? . . .

Ask the question, "Why is it so hard sometimes to see and say good things about ourselves?" and invite responses from the young people.

Tell them that you are challenging them to acknowledge the good in themselves. On their poster they are to write four to six gifts and positive qualities they possess. They should write them near the related body part. For example, they could write "great listener" by the ears, or "good at building things" near the hands. Qualities that cannot be connected to a body part can be written anywhere on the body. Caution them to avoid superficial characteristics such as, "I have nice eyes," or "I have good taste in clothes." If you created a model before the session, show them your silhouette.

Allow about 5 minutes for this part of the process. Keep close track of time. When they are finished, they should tape their poster to a wall.

4. When everyone has posted a silhouette, gather the young people in a group facing the posters. Make the following comments in your own words:

> Just as it is often difficult to recognize our own gifts and talents, we some-times find it tough to say positive things about one another. We make jokes about people and often put them down. We have all been hurt by other people's comments, and we have probably all hurt someone else with ours.

Ask the question, "Why is it so hard to see the good in others and tell them and other people about the good you see?" Again invite responses.

Explain that the young teens will have a chance to affirm and encourage one another. They are to walk around the room and write on people's posters some of the gifts and positive qualities they see in them. If the quality can be connected to a body part, they should write it near that part. If not they can write it anywhere on the inside of the body.

Allow about 15 minutes for this process. If you are working with a small group of young people, invite them to write on each person's poster. If you have a large group, you may want to ask them to start by affirming the people in their small group or the ones that are on the same wall as theirs before they move on to others.

5. Allow a few minutes for the teens to read the comments added to their own poster. Then close the activity by urging them to continue finding the good in themselves and celebrating that good, and also to look for and acknowledge the good in other people. At all times they should avoid put-downs and com-ments that can hurt others.

Allow the young people to take their posters home. Suggest that they hang them in their room and read them whenever they feel like God's only mistake.

6. Conclude the session by reading 1 Cor. 12:12–31, emphasizing that each part of the body is unique and serves a different purpose in making the whole body function properly. So too are we—as members of the Body of Christ— unique and important.

ALTERNATIVE APPROACHES

- ◎ If you do not have space available for life-size posters, give everyone a sheet of poster board and ask them to draw a silhouette of their partner or their own silhouette. Proceed with the activity in the same manner as above.
- ◎ If time is available, invite the young people to "dress" and decorate their body posters. Make a variety of markers, colored paper, and other craft items available.
- ◎ Keep the posters up for a while and invite people to add to them at subsequent sessions.
- ◎ At the end of the session, give each young person a 5-by-8-inch index card. Tell them to draw the figure of a person on the card and write "Here I am!" at the top. During the week they should write at least one positive thing about themselves each day. Invite them to introduce themselves at a later session by reading off the list of additional qualities.
- ◎ If you are doing this activity as part of a retreat or an extended session, form the young people into small groups, give each group a Bible, and ask them to create a skit dramatizing 1 Cor. 12:12–31.

SCRIPTURAL CONNECTIONS

- ◎ 1 Cor. 12:4–11 (We have many gifts, but the same spirit.)
- ◎ Jer. 1:4–10 (Do not say that you are too young.)
- ◎ Psalm 139 (God's works are marvelous.)

NOTES

Use the space below to jot notes and reminders for the next time you use this strategy.

Take Me Out to the Ball Game

A Reflection and Discussion Exercise

This activity is designed to spark discussion on the attitudes young teens bring with them to Mass, using the image of a baseball game for comparison. It encourages them to participate fully and to do their part to make celebrating the Sunday liturgy meaningful for everyone.

Suggested Time

10 to 20 minutes

Group Size

This strategy works best with groups of fewer than forty teens.

Materials Needed

- ☼ copies of handout 1, "Take Me Out to the Ball Game," one for each person
- ☼ pens or pencils
- ☼ newsprint and markers

PROCEDURE

1. Distribute a copy of handout 1 and a pen or pencil to each person. Ask the young people to think about the attitudes they bring with them when they attend Mass on Sunday. Encourage them to be honest and not just say what they think you want them to say.

2. Challenge the young people to compare their attitude toward Mass to a baseball game. Ask them to draw a stick figure on the handout to represent themselves and their attitude toward Mass right now. You might want to give examples such as these:

I placed myself in the locker room because I would rather stay home, but my parents make me come.

I placed myself in the grandstand because I watch what is going on, but I really don't understand Mass all that much.

I placed myself at shortstop because I know I've got to pay attention to everything that's going on.

3. Next, invite the young people to indicate where they would like to see themselves. They should add another stick figure, this time one wearing a baseball cap. Give examples such as these:

I would like to be on the pitcher's mound because I want to grow closer to God every time I go to Mass.

I would like to be at the gate to the stadium, inviting other people to come to Mass and making them feel welcome.

Invite them to share their responses with a partner or in a small group of three people.

4. Gather the teens into one group and plan your strategy for the next inning. Invite them to brainstorm answers to the question, "What can you do to get more out of Mass each time you go?" List their answers on newsprint.

ALTERNATIVE APPROACHES

◎ If time permits, add the question: What can our parish do to include youth and make them feel more welcome at Mass? Share this discussion with your pastor and liturgy planning committee.

◎ If you have access to a real baseball diamond on your school or parish property, or if there is a ballpark nearby, try the first part of this activity by allowing the young people to actually go out and stand in the spot that represents how they feel about going to Mass.

◎ Create a simulated ball field in a gym, cafeteria, or an open space. Use masking tape to mark the baselines, the bleachers as the stadium seats, pillows for bases, and so forth. Have the young people move around, depending on their response to your questions.

SCRIPTURAL CONNECTIONS

◎ Luke 24:28–34 (Jesus is recognized in the breaking of the bread.)
◎ Acts 2:43–47 (Life among the early Christians)
◎ Acts 20:7–12 (The story of Eutychus)

NOTES

Use the space below to jot notes and reminders for the next time you use this strategy.

Take Me Out
to the Ball Game

Think about the attitudes you bring with you when you attend Sunday Mass. compare your attitude toward Mass to a baseball game. Draw a stick figure on the diagram below to represent yourself and your attitude toward Mass right now.

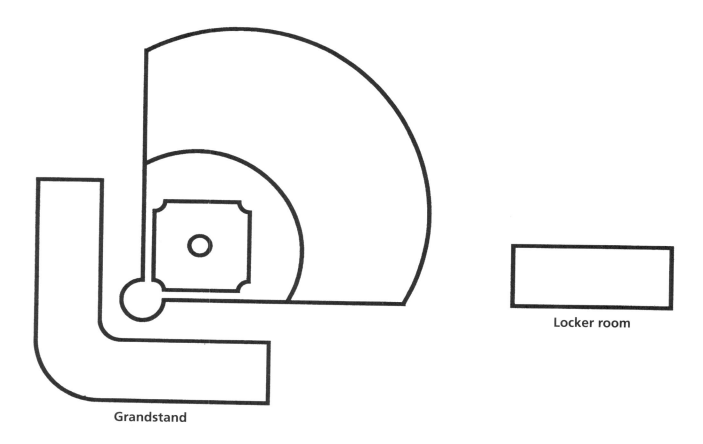

Locker room

Grandstand

Part B
Active Learning Strategies

The activities in this section are designed to jump-start the learning process by engaging the young people in an active and meaningful way. Most of the strategies can be adapted and used for a variety of topics. If young adolescents move through an active lesson, they are more likely to remember it. This section also contains several techniques for reviewing material and checking progress.

Church Search

Church Tour
and Vocabulary Lesson

OVERVIEW

This strategy gives the young teens an opportunity to explore, touch, and reverence their church. At the same time, it teaches them relevant vocabulary and familiarizes them not only with common objects found in all churches but also with the unique characteristics of their own worship space.

Suggested Time

45 to 60 minutes

Group Size

This strategy works best with groups of twenty teens or fewer. If you have more than twenty, you may want to recruit other adults and do the tour simultaneously, but starting in different places.

Special Considerations

The young people may be interested in seeing where items such as chalices, communion plates, communion hosts, and so forth are kept in the sacristy. However, if you do not have the authority to explore the sacristy, get permission to do so or ask a priest or parish staff member to lead the group through this area.

Materials Needed

- ☼ index cards
- ☼ markers

PROCEDURE

Preparation. Before the tour be sure that items that will be on the search and tour are available and obvious. For example, if the lectionary is regularly kept in a locked cupboard, ask a church staff member to leave it out for the session.

Decide on a route for the church tour that will cover all the items and spaces included in the search.

Write each of the following words or phrases on an index card. Add names of other significant items and areas in your worship space or seasonal symbols such as an Advent wreath or banners. Delete those items that are not applicable or accessible in your worship space.

◎ ambo	◎ balcony
◎ altar	◎ baptismal font
◎ presider's chair	◎ sanctuary
◎ lectern	◎ sanctuary candle
◎ tabernacle	◎ sacristy
◎ stained-glass windows	◎ confessional
◎ holy oils	◎ holy water font
◎ incense	◎ lectionary
◎ censer	◎ mission cross
◎ sacramentary	◎ vestments
◎ gathering space	◎ stations of the cross
◎ paschal candle	◎ statues (by name)
◎ candles	

1. Gather the young people at the church entrance. Randomly and evenly distribute the index cards with the names of items and places in the church. Tell the participants that when you give the signal, they are to place each card on or near the item named on the card. As they do so, they are to think about why that item is significant for their parish community or their worship life. If they have questions about a certain item, they can ask a peer or an adult for help.

Allow enough time for the young people to place all their cards. If you have a large group and each person has only one card, allow only about 2 minutes. If each person has five cards, allow about 10 minutes. Announce how much time they have to place the cards. Tell them that when they finish or when time is up, they are to return to the starting point and give you any cards that they could not place.

Give the signal for the church search to begin. When time is up, call it and regather the group at the church entrance.

2. Lead the group on a tour of the church. Be sure to stop at every site that has a card. Ask the person who placed the card to tell the group why he or she thinks the object or place is significant for the parish or what the function of it might be. You may need to help the person or open the question to the entire group.

If any cards were returned to you, add them to the tour and describe their function or significance yourself.

ALTERNATIVE APPROACHES

◎ Collect the cards and use them for review in a later session.
◎ Include the presider's garments in the tour. You might even have one or more of the teens try on the garments. Be sure, however, that your pastor is aware of this and agreeable to it. Invite him to explain what each of the garments means.
◎ Assign one object or part of the church to each young person and ask her or him to research the origins of each item or the process by which it was acquired. For example, assign one person to research the architect of the church, another to research the artist who did the stained-glass windows, another to check out how and from where the parish gets hosts and wine, and so forth. This project will take time and can be done over several weeks, depending on how elaborate it gets. It will also involve work in the parish library, conversations with the pastor or parish librarian, and even some research into historical documents. It could also involve a trip to a stained-glass studio or the religious goods store, or a conversation with the curator of the local historical society. Depending on how far you want to take this project, it might be a good project for a young person and an adult to do together over a span of time.

NOTES

Use the space below to jot notes and reminders for the next time you use this strategy.

The Journeys of Jesus
A Lesson on Biblical Travels

Using biblical maps the young people calculate the approximate mileage Jesus walked and compare it with distances in their locale. This is an ideal activity to use as part of a lesson or a retreat on the ministry of Jesus.

Suggested Time

30 to 40 minutes

Group Size

This strategy works well with up to thirty-five people.

Special Considerations

For this strategy you will need a Bible that includes a map of the Holy Land in the time of Jesus, identifying the places that were significant in Jesus' life. Most study editions of the Bible include this information. *The Catholic Youth Bible* (Winona, MN: Saint Mary's Press, 2000) is an excellent resource for this material. If you do not have Bibles available, several publishers and vendors of religious education materials sell larger maps.

Materials Needed

- handout 2, "Jesus' Journeys," one for each person
- Bibles with maps of Jesus' travels, one for each person, or large poster maps
- pencils
- rulers, one for every two or three people
- local maps, one for every two or three people
- notebook paper
- calculators (optional)

PROCEDURE

1. Ask the young people to name some of the towns that they associate with the life of Jesus. They are likely to come up Jerusalem, Bethlehem, Nazareth, or Emmaus. Point out that Jesus walked wherever he went and always talked with others as he walked.

Divide the group into pairs or triads. Give each person a copy of handout 2, a Bible, a pencil, a ruler, a local map, and a sheet of notebook paper. If you have calculators available, distribute them at this time also.

2. Announce to the teens that they are going to calculate the distance that Jesus traveled during the three years of his ministry. Point out the map in the Bible (or on the poster) and explain the type of information that is included in the map. Be sure to point out the mileage scale. Do the same for the map of your local area.

3. Assign each small group one or more of the following journeys from handout 2:

- Bethlehem (the place of Jesus' birth) to Nazareth (the place where he grew up) (Luke 2:39–40)
- Nazareth (his family home) to Jerusalem (the Temple, where he became separated from his parents) (Luke 2:39–51)
- Nazareth to Cana (his first miracle, at a wedding feast) (John 2:1–11)
- Cana to Capernaum (after the wedding feast) (John 2:12)
- Capernaum to Jerusalem (for Passover) (John 2:12–14)
- Jerusalem to Bethabara or Salim (where John was baptizing) (John 3:22–23)
- Bethsaida (where he cured a blind man) to Caesarea Philippi (Mark 8:22–30)
- Jerusalem to Sychar (where he talked to the Samaritan woman) (John 4:7–26)
- Sidon to the Sea of Galilee (Matt. 15:21–29)
- Bethsaida (where he cured a blind man) to Mount Tabor (site of the Transfiguration) (Mark 8:22; 9:2–8)

4. Explain the following process for finding, calculating, and comparing distances:

Find the two places mentioned in the example.

Measure the distance (in inches) between the two points.

Using the mileage scale, figure out how many miles Jesus and his family or friends had to walk to get from one place to the other.

If he took a leisurely pace of approximately three miles per hour, how long did it take him to get to his destination? For example, if Jesus' destination was 30 miles from his starting point, it would have taken him 10 hours to walk.

Look at the local map. Find your approximate location. Then, using the mileage scale on the local map, figure out where a person would go to walk a comparable distance in the same direction. For example, if Jesus' journey meant walking 90 miles south, what town is approximately 90 miles south of your location?

Look up the passages that are associated with the journey. Read the journey passages and the material that comes before and after them. Find out what Jesus did along the way from one place to the other.

5. After the groups have finished their calculations, bring them together and have them compare their findings. Add up the total miles that result, and announce the total number of miles that Jesus walked on the journeys that they researched. Remind the teens that Jesus went on many more journeys with his disciples than they calculated, and that he did it all in three years.

ALTERNATIVE APPROACHES

◎ Use the same process to calculate the journeys of Paul or the Israelites' Exodus from Egypt through the desert to Mount Nebo, the place where Moses died.

◎ To extend this lesson over a longer period of time, begin by having the young people look up Jesus' journeys themselves. Assign each person a certain section of, for example, Matthew's Gospel. Tell them to read through the passage and find mention of any places that Jesus traveled through or stopped at. Have them find these locations on a map and measure the distance Jesus traveled. They should also figure out who Jesus was with, what he did on the way, and where he stopped.

Follow this activity with "Wander and Ponder" from part A. Make the point that even though we are not accustomed to walking long distances, we can do many things in the places where we are that will also spread joy, peace, and healing.

NOTES

Use the space below to jot notes and reminders for the next time you use this strategy.

Jesus' Journeys

Your leader will assign you to one of Jesus' journeys listed below. For the journey you are assigned, complete the following steps:

◎ Find on a map the two places mentioned.

◎ Measure the distance (in inches) between the two points.

◎ Using the mileage scale, figure out how many miles Jesus and his family or friends had to walk to get from one place to the other.

◎ If he took a leisurely pace of approximately three miles per hour, how long did it take him to get to his destination? For example, if Jesus' destination was 30 miles from his starting point, it would have taken him 10 hours to walk.

◎ Look at the local map. Find your approximate location. Then, using the mileage scale on the local map, figure out where a person would have go to walk a comparable distance in the same direction. For example, if Jesus' journey meant walking 90 miles south, what town is approximately 90 miles south of your location?

◎ Look up the passages that are associated with the journey. Read the journey passages and the material that comes before and after them. Find out what Jesus did along the way from one place to the other.

1. Bethlehem (the place of Jesus' birth) to Nazareth (the place where he grew up) (Luke 2:39–40)

2. Nazareth (his family home) to Jerusalem (the Temple, where he became separated from his parents) (Luke 2:39–51)

3. Nazareth to Cana (his first miracle, at a wedding feast) (John 2:1–11)

4. Cana to Capernaum (after the wedding feast) (John 2:12)

5. Capernaum to Jerusalem (for Passover) (John 2:12–14)

6. Jerusalem to Bethabara or Salim (where John was baptizing) (John 3:22–23)

7. Bethsaida (where he cured a blind man) to Caesarea Philippi (Mark 8:22–30)

8. Jerusalem to Sychar (where he talked to the Samaritan woman) (John 4:7–26)

9. Sidon to the Sea of Galilee (Matt. 15:21–29)

10. Bethsaida (where he cured a blind man) to Mount Tabor (site of the Transfiguration) (Mark 8:22, 9:2–8)

Line It Up
A Timeline
Learning Activity

This timeline activity is a fun way to learn or review dates and events in church history, in the Bible, or in the history of the parish. It is active, visual, hands-on, and an ideal addition to a religious education class.

Suggested Time

25 to 40 minutes, depending on the number of events and dates

Group Size

This strategy works best with between ten and forty young teens. A suggestion for adapting the activity for a small group is described in the alternative approaches section.

Materials Needed

- ☼ 4-by-6-inch index cards, two for each date in the timeline
- ☼ markers
- ☼ a clothesline or twine
- ☼ spring-clip clothespins, one per person

PROCEDURE

Preparation. Write each date from your timeline on a separate index card. Write the events or the significance of those dates on another set of cards.

String clothesline or twine from one side of the room to the other, high enough so that the young people can reach the line but not interfere with it.

1. Randomly distribute the index cards you created before the session. Explain to the teens that they will create a timeline of events and dates with their cards. Their task is to find the person with the card that complements theirs so that the event and the date match. Allow a few minutes for each person to find his or her partner.

2. When everyone has found their partner, direct the teens to line up according to the sequence of dates. After they line up, ask them to read the dates and events in sequence. Encourage them to challenge one another if they think a pairing is inaccurate or out of sequence.

3. Give everyone a clothespin and tell them to clip their card to the line. Date cards should come before the events they apply to. Leave the timeline up until you finish the unit. Have the young people add other events to the timeline as they learn them.

ALTERNATIVE APPROACHES

◎ If you have a small group, mix up the cards and lay them out on the floor. Have the teens take turns finding an event and a date that match and hanging it on the proper place on the line.

◎ Once the timeline has been up for a while, take it down for a few days. To review the material at a subsequent session, reshuffle the cards and distribute them. Have the teens follow the same process as above.

◎ Use the same technique for any material that requires knowing a sequence. You may or may not be able to use the pairs, depending on the nature of the material. Use the process for learning or reviewing facts like the sequence of books of the Bible or the seasons and events in the liturgical year.

◎ Instead of clipping the cards to a clothesline, tape them to an empty wall. If you cannot leave the cards up between sessions, purchase a continuous roll of paper, such as shelf paper, and tape the cards to the paper. Remove it after each session and replace it before the next.

◎ If the young people are not real familiar with the material, make textbooks, resource books, and other sources of information available. Be aware that doing so may significantly lengthen the activity, however.

NOTES

Use the space below to jot notes and reminders for the next time you use this strategy.

KGOD Eyewitness News Nazareth

A Television Interview Simulation

This strategy puts young people in the roles of newscasters and reporters who have been sent out to interview the friends of Jesus. In the process of creating the news story, they must find out everything they can about their character from the Gospel.

Suggested Time

About an hour for planning, an hour or more for preparation, and the actual time it takes to "broadcast" the interview. This strategy can be done over the course of several sessions or on a retreat.

Group Size

This strategy works best with groups of fifteen or fewer participants.

Special Considerations

This project involves a good deal of time, energy, and creativity on the part of the participants. You may want to invite to the "broadcast" parish staff, parents, other teens, or anyone else who will appreciate the effort of these young people.

Materials Needed

- ☼ newsprint and markers
- ☼ masking tape
- ☼ Bibles, one for each person
- ☼ paper
- ☼ pens or pencils
- ☼ craft supplies
- ☼ skit supplies
- ☼ poster board
- ☼ a video camera and a blank videotape (optional)

PROCEDURE

Preparation. Decide which Gospel figures you want to be part of the TV simulation. Choose prominent characters. Several are listed below, but you can choose any that the participants might find interesting to learn more about. List the names on newsprint and post it.

- ◎ Peter
- ◎ Mary of Magdala
- ◎ the Samaritan woman at the well
- ◎ Nicodemus
- ◎ John the Baptist
- ◎ John the Apostle
- ◎ Matthew
- ◎ Judas
- ◎ a Pharisee
- ◎ Jairus, whose daughter Jesus healed
- ◎ Mary, Martha, and Lazarus
- ◎ Pontius Pilate
- ◎ a member of the Sanhedrin
- ◎ one of the ten lepers
- ◎ the boy whose loaves and fish fed five thousand

1. Present the following scenario to the group in your own words:

It's about the year A.D. 32. A man called Jesus of Nazareth is causing quite a stir among the residents of towns between the Sea of Galilee and Jerusalem. You received a call from TV station KGOD, also known as Eyewitness News Nazareth. They want to do a story on this hometown celebrity. They can handle the interviews in Nazareth, but they asked you to find a couple of reporters to interview people who got to know Jesus after he left Nazareth— his friends and his enemies.

2. Display the newsprint list of biblical characters that you created before the session. Announce that you will need two or three reporters for these interviews. Everyone else will take the role of someone being interviewed. You will serve as anchorperson. Explain the preparation tasks as follows:

The task of the reporters is to find out enough about the people they will be interviewing to ask intelligent questions.

The task of the interviewees is to find out enough about their character from the Gospel stories so that they can accurately represent this person. What they do not learn from the Gospels they can make up, but it has to be in character.

Assign each person a role based on his or her preferences.

2. Distribute Bibles, paper, and pens or pencils. For those who are representing specific characters, tell them that their task is to find as many references to their character as possible, read the passages, and write the citations on the paper for future reference. You may need to help some people find information on certain people. When they are done, they should have a fairly clear picture of who the person is, what she or he does for a living, what her or his relationship with Jesus is like, how she or he feels about Jesus, and so forth.

Assign each of the reporters a few characters. Tell them to come up with a list of questions they would like to ask the interviewees to make for an interesting news story. They too can search the Gospels for information on the characters. Ask the characters to share their list of biblical citations with the reporters.

3. At a future session or later in the event, work with the group to design the interview program. Suggest the following parameters for the program:

The entire show should not be more than 30 minutes long, but not less than 15 minutes.

Each character should be interviewed for factual information as well as for information about his or her relationship with Jesus.

At the end of the news program, people should have a better idea of who Jesus really is, as seen through the eyes of his friends and enemies.

Allow the teens to be as creative as they can be. They may want to think of a title for the show and use props and costumes. Provide craft supplies, sign-making supplies, and various supplies for skits. They may even want to do commercials for fictional places and products, such as "Jerusalem Toga Outlet," "Rent-a-Donkey," or "Peter's Fresh Fish House." Let their imaginations run wild—within the bounds of your time limits. Suggest that they continue their work at home.

4. Allow time for rehearsal before the teens do their final take. You may want to videotape the news show and play the tape for the group later.

ALTERNATIVE APPROACHES

◎ The role of the anchor is really the role of the director. If someone in your group wants to take on that role and organize the production, give him or her the chance to do it.
◎ If someone from your parish works in television or video production, invite her or him to be part of the project.
◎ Recruit other adults to each supervise a few young people. The adults could be around to help them find passages related to the character and turn the passages into a newsworthy script.
◎ Use the same technique when the young people study various biblical figures, such as David, Moses, or Paul.

NOTES

Use the space below to jot notes and reminders for the next time you use this strategy.

Know Your Scripture

An Activity to Memorize Scripture Verses

Memorizing verses from the Scriptures can be a challenge for young teens. This strategy provides an active and fun way for them to commit important verses to memory.

Suggested Time

5 to 15 minutes, depending on the number of verses

Group Size

This strategy works best with groups of eight or more teens.

Materials Needed

- index cards (preferably in several colors)
- markers
- a box or bag
- Bibles
- small prizes or treats (optional)

PROCEDURE

Preparation. Choose a scriptural verse and write each word of the verse on a separate index card. Use verses related to lessons you are teaching, verses from the Sunday readings, or ones that are seasonally appropriate. Include articles with their nouns, for example, use one card for "the light" rather than separating "the" and "light." Include the biblical citation on a separate card. Put all the cards in a box or bag.

Prepare enough verses so that every person in the group has one card. If you have a large group, or if the young people are not familiar with many scriptural verses, you may want to use a different color of index card for each verse.

1. Pass the bag or box of cards around the group and have each person choose one card. Ask the people who are holding citation cards to hold them up, and announce that the cards everyone else is holding belong to one of the scriptural citations. Explain that the task is to find everyone who has a word that is part of that verse and arrange the words in order. The group that arranges their verse correctly first wins.

2. Keep track of the order in which the groups finish the task. When all the verses are complete, give each group a Bible and have them look up their verse to see if it is accurate. After everyone has checked, ask each group to read its quote aloud by having each person in the group read his or her own word in order. They should face the other groups with their cards visible. When they finish reading, invite the entire group to read the quote in unison.

Name the group that was the first to finish correctly as the winner. You may want to award small prizes or treats to each group member.

ALTERNATIVE APPROACHES

◎ Instead of doing several quotes at one time, just do one at a time. Call forth the same number of people as you have cards and distribute the cards randomly. Have them arrange themselves in order. Ask someone who is not in the group to check the quotations against a Bible to ensure accuracy.

◎ If you are working with a small group, put phrases instead of words on the cards so that fewer people will be needed to complete a verse.

◎ If the young people in your group are not familiar with the scriptural verses you are using, you may want to provide copies of the Bible for their reference. Be sure that the edition you give the teens is the same one that you used for the quotes.

◎ Instead of giving each person a card, place all the cards faceup on the floor or on a table. Challenge the teens to put the cards together to form verses. This works particularly well if you have a small group.

◎ At the end of the session, ask the young people to gather again with their verse group in the proper order. This time do not allow them to use the cards. Ask each person in turn to recite his or her word. At the end ask the verse group to recite the whole verse together, followed by a recitation from the large group. You might also do this at the next class or session.

NOTES

Use the space below to jot notes and reminders for the next time you use this strategy.

Spotlight
on the Sacraments
Discussion and Presentation

OVERVIEW

This activity challenges the young people to find a creative way to think about what the sacraments mean and how they connect with everyday life. The young people choose their own form of expression by which to share their understanding of one of the sacraments. This is an ideal activity for a course on the sacraments, the church, or Confirmation preparation.

Suggested Time

About 30 minutes of planning time plus 3 to 5 minutes per group for the presentations

Group Size

This strategy works with any size group, but the teens will work in small groups of six to eight participants.

Materials Needed

- :Ö: newsprint and markers
- :Ö: assorted craft supplies
- :Ö: assorted skit supplies
- :Ö: a portable spotlight

PROCEDURE

Preparation. Write the following questions on newsprint:

- What is the sacrament about?
- What does it have to do with us today?
- How does this sacrament communicate God's love for us?

1. Ask the young teens to name the seven sacraments of the church. As they do so, list them on newsprint. Fill in any blanks if they have trouble naming all seven.

2. Choose one of the sacraments and lead a discussion around the following questions:

What is this sacrament about?

What does it have to do with us today?

How does this sacrament communicate God's love for us?

3. Form the teens into small groups of six to eight people. Assign each group a sacrament to spotlight. Display the questions that you wrote on newsprint, and tell the participants to discuss with their small group the questions about the sacrament they were assigned, in much the same way as the large group did earlier. Allow 5 to 10 minutes for this discussion.

4. Announce that each group will have a chance to put its sacrament in the spotlight by creatively presenting it. In this way everyone will learn more about it and better understand God's gift to Catholic Christians.

Give the young people the following examples, but allow them to add their own creative ideas. Tell them that as a group they can create any of the following:

a poem

a skit

a Web page

a television commercial

a song (or change the words to an existing song)

a debate

a human sculpture

a poster

a crossword puzzle

Make the craft items and skit props available to the group. Allow about 30 minutes for the teens to come up with ideas and do the work.

5. Assign each group to a spot in the room for its presentation. Turn off all the lights in your meeting space except for your portable spotlight. As each group makes its presentation, direct the spotlight to that group's area.

6. Close by challenging the young people to continue learning more about the sacraments and how they can have an impact on each of our lives.

ALTERNATIVE APPROACHES

- If you are doing this activity as part of a sacraments course, you may want to spotlight a different sacrament each week. Give the teens a few options each week (from the list in step 4) and time to come up with a creative presentation.
- Use this same idea to put the spotlight on different saints, seasons of the liturgical year, books of the Bible, phrases from the Nicene Creed or the Lord's Prayer, or any other material that the young people need to learn and understand.

NOTES

Use the space below to jot notes and reminders for the next time you use this strategy.

Sacraments Mobile
A Craft and Discussion Exercise

The seven sacraments of the Catholic church are rich in symbolism that can offer clues on ways to better understand the mysteries of our faith. This activity invites the young teens to create a mobile by which they identify symbols and words to describe each sacrament.

Suggested Time

45 to 60 minutes

Group Size

This activity works with any size group, but the teens will work in smaller groups of six to eight people. Be sure to have enough adult supervision.

Materials Needed

- ☼ newsprint and markers
- ☼ a copy of resource 1, "The Seven Sacraments," cut apart as scored
- ☼ a bag
- ☼ hangers, one for each group
- ☼ yarn, one ball for each group

☼ old magazines, several for each group
☼ scissors, one for each group
☼ glue, one bottle for each group
☼ poster board, one sheet for each group
☼ other craft supplies (optional)
☼ hole punches

PROCEDURE

Preparation. Create a sample mobile before the session so that you can explain the process better and head off any difficulties.

Make a copy of resource 1 and cut out as many sets as you need for the size of your group. Cut apart the lists and put them in a bag.

1. Ask the young people to identify the seven sacraments. As they do so, list the sacraments on newsprint. When they have listed all seven sacraments, ask them if they can identify at least one symbol for each of the sacraments.

2. Pass around the bag with the names of the sacraments that you prepared before the session. Tell the young people to randomly pick a slip of paper. When everyone has one, announce that they are to form a group of seven with everyone's paper naming a different sacrament. If the number of teens in your group is not a multiple of seven, some groups may consist of either six people (in which case one of the sacraments would not be represented) or eight (a sacrament is repeated).

3. Distribute to each small group a hanger, some yarn, some used magazines, a scissors, a bottle of glue, a piece of poster board, and other craft supplies. Explain that each small group is to create a mobile using symbols that communicate something about each of the seven sacraments. Outline the following process in your own words:

The mobile must contain one piece for each sacrament. The piece can include one symbol or many symbols. The pieces can be cut from poster board, or words and pictures can be cut out of old magazines and mounted on poster board. Official church symbols may be used, such as water, oil, rings, and so forth. Other symbols can also be used. For example, for the sacrament of Baptism, you may cut out a picture of a stream because water is a symbol of Baptism, or you may cut out pictures of babies because many people are baptized as infants. In other words the symbols need not be formal ones connected with the sacrament, but any pictures that help you communicate what the sacrament means.

After all seven pieces are finished, punch a hole in the top of each piece and attach it with yarn to the hanger. Vary the lengths of yarn, so it will be easier to see each sacrament when the mobile is hanging.

4. Allow about 25 minutes for the groups to work on their mobile. When all the groups are finished, invite a spokesperson from each group to explain its mobile to the larger group.

Find a place to display the mobiles in your regular gathering space or a prominent place in your school or parish.

ALTERNATIVE APPROACHES

◎ You may want to consult another volume in the HELP series, *Community-Building Activities for Ministry with Young Teens,* for creative suggestions for forming small groups.

◎ Instead of the entire small group working on the mobile, assign each person one sacrament. Allow time for them each to work on their piece, and ask them to share the contents of their piece as the mobile is being assembled.

◎ If you have seven small groups of teens, ask each group to work on one sacrament or one mobile piece and assemble a large mobile for your class or youth group. Instead of a hanger, use a long dowel so that you have more room to hang the pieces.

◎ If you are using this activity as part of a course on sacraments that meets over several weeks, create a mobile piece each week with the goal of completing the mobile by the end of the course.

◎ Allow the young people to cut out words as well as pictures from the magazines in describing what the sacrament means to them.

◎ This is an ideal activity for the teens to work on with young children who are studying the sacraments for the first time. The children will appreciate connecting with the young teens, and the teens will benefit from having to explain the sacraments to children in the most basic terms.

NOTES

Use the space below to jot notes and reminders for the next time you use this strategy.

The Seven Sacraments

Cut apart as many sets of sacraments as you need so that each person gets one slip of paper.

Baptism	Baptism	Baptism
Reconciliation	Reconciliation	Reconciliation
Eucharist	Eucharist	Eucharist
Confirmation	Confirmation	Confirmation
Marriage	Marriage	Marriage
Holy Orders	Holy Orders	Holy Orders
Anointing of the Sick	Anointing of the Sick	Anointing of the Sick

Jackpot!

A Review Activity

Reviewing material can be tedious and tension-filled. This strategy provides a fun and active way to review a lesson. It also gives the leader a chance to reinforce learning. The activity can be used with any material that must be remembered.

Suggested Time

About 3 minutes. Longer if the leader decides to keep it going and has enough material to do so.

Group Size

This strategy works with any size group. If you have more than about fifteen in your group, break into smaller groups and do the activity in each group simultaneously. You will need an adult leader involved with each small group.

Materials Needed

- ☼ a Nerf ball, rolled socks, or something else that is soft and can be tossed around safely
- ☼ review questions on individual papers or cards
- ☼ a box or bag

PROCEDURE

Preparation. Type out a series of review questions based on the material you have covered in your sessions. Cut apart the questions and put them in a bag or box. If you are doing this activity with several groups simultaneously, you will need one set of questions for each group.

1. Gather the young people in a circle and give someone a Nerf ball, rolled up socks, or anything else that is soft and can be thrown around safely. Explain the process in your own words as follows:

> When the leader gives the signal, the person with the ball tosses it to anyone else in the group, who tosses it to someone else, who tosses it to someone else, and so forth.

> The leader will periodically call out "Jackpot!" Whoever has the ball at that point pulls a question from the bag or box and answers it.

> If that person answers correctly, he or she tosses the ball to someone else and then steps out of the circle. If he or she answers incorrectly, he or she tosses the ball but stays in the circle. Play continues until someone answers correctly.

> The person who answers correctly steps out of the circle and turns his or her back to the circle. This person becomes the one to say "Jackpot." His or her turn continues until someone else answers a question correctly and takes over the role of calling "Jackpot."

2. Give the signal to begin tossing the ball. Turn your back to the group and call out "Jackpot" after a few seconds. Follow the process as it is outlined above. Continue until everyone has answered a question correctly, until all the questions are gone, or until time is up.

ALTERNATIVE APPROACHES

 Instead of writing the review questions yourself, distribute index cards to the teens, and ask them to write one or more questions on the material studied. Then follow the same process to review the material using the questions submitted.

NOTES

Use the space below to jot notes and reminders for the next time you use this strategy.

Snowball Fight

An Icebreaker and Timeline Exercise

This strategy gives the young teens a history of your parish and builds pride in the parish community. At the same time, it gets them up and active. It is a good activity to use at the beginning of a class or session because it begins with an icebreaker. It is also a good way to energize a group in the middle of a class or retreat.

Suggested Time

30 to 45 minutes

Group Size

This strategy works with any size group.

Special Considerations

Young teens can get carried away with the first part of this strategy, putting themselves at risk of injury if the room is cluttered with furniture. This activity works best in a room with few obstacles and a lot of blank wall space. A gym or cafeteria is ideal.

Materials Needed

- ☼ 8½-by-11-inch paper, two blank sheets per person plus extras
- ☼ markers
- ☼ masking tape
- ☼ old magazines and newspapers
- ☼ scissors
- ☼ a variety of craft supplies

PROCEDURE

Preparation. Create a timeline of the history of your parish. Include its beginnings, consecration, leaders, organizations, people, building projects, major events, anniversary celebrations, or anything else that will give the young people a sense of the history of their parish. You might include fun things, like the year the pastor was born, your own Baptism date, or the years most of the young people would have been baptized or received their first Eucharist. Try to have at least one event per person.

Write each date on a separate piece of plain paper. Wad up the papers to resemble snowballs.

1. Give each person a snowball. If you have more snowballs than young people, give some more than one. Explain that at the signal, they are to begin throwing the balls to one another. Emphasize that they should throw the balls *to* and not *at* one another. The task is to keep all the snowballs off the ground. If a snowball hits them and falls to the ground, they must pick it up and throw it to someone else.

After about a minute, stop the snowball fight. Make sure everyone has a snowball and that all the snowballs are accounted for. If you have more snow-balls than teens in your group, distribute the extras randomly.

Explain that the activity was more than a way to burn off some energy. The snowballs that they were throwing around contain the history of their parish. Tell the teens to open their snowball and smooth it out. Provide everyone with two pieces of masking tape and have them tape their date(s) on the wall in numerical order. Tell them to remember which date or dates were theirs.

2. When all the dates are posted, go through the timeline and give a brief history of the parish. Describe for the group the significance of each date.

3. Give the participants each a sheet of blank paper and tell them to write at the top of the paper the event or significance of the date they posted. (If they posted more than one date, they may choose one.) Make markers, magazines, newspapers, and other craft supplies available. Tell the teens that they are to create a pictorial history of the parish. Explain that for the date they posted, they

must draw a symbol, find a picture in a magazine, or otherwise create something that represents that event. Some people may want to go around the church and draw things like the cornerstone, do a rubbing of a plaque on the wall of the new addition (by putting a piece of paper over it and going over it lightly with a crayon), or get a leaf or a piece of bark from the tree that was planted the year the church was built.

When they finish their picture, they are to tape it below the date on the wall.

4. When everyone has completed the task, congratulate the teens on creating a quick reference to the history of the parish. If possible, move the time-line to a place in the parish where it can be viewed and enjoyed by everyone.

ALTERNATIVE APPROACHES

- If your community has a parish historian, invite him or her to be present and tell the story of the parish. The historian may be able to answer many of the teens' questions that you may not be able to.
- If you do not have a large expanse of blank wall space, lay out on the floor a long strip of rolled butcher paper, newsprint, or shelf paper. Have the young people tape their date and picture to the paper on the floor. When you are finished, have a number of teens carry the timeline carefully to a space where they can post it for general viewing.
- To save time, write the events and dates on the papers. After the young people post the dates in order, briefly review the historical information.
- This strategy works well with any timeline and sequence material. For example, you could use it to review dates in church history or the order of books in the Bible.
- Use the snowball fight as a team game. Form two groups and string up a "net" separating them. For the net, you could hang a rope between two chairs and put a sheet over it.

  Divide the snowballs equally between the two groups. The object of the game is to be the team with the fewest snowballs on its side of the net. Tell the young people that they must stay seated throughout the game. If someone moves from a seated position, you will stop the game and move five snowballs to the side of the offending team.

  Allow the game to go on for a minute or two before moving on to the review part of the activity.

NOTES

Use the space below to jot notes and reminders for the next time you use this strategy.

Popcorn
A Review Exercise

This strategy is a fun, light, quick, and noisy way to review lessons by putting questions into balloons and having the young people pop them and answer the question. It can be used with any material in any curriculum.

Suggested Time

5 to 10 minutes

Group Size

This strategy works with any size group, but if your group is large, divide it into smaller groups. Have enough adult supervision on hand to help with the small groups.

Materials Needed

☀ uninflated balloons, 9 inches or more in diameter, one for each young person, in equal numbers of different colors

☀ review questions written on slips of paper, one for each young person

☀ a bag or box

PROCEDURE

Preparation. Type out questions based on the lesson you want to review. Be sure to have at least one question for every person. Cut the questions apart, fold them, and place them in a bag or box.

Purchase party-size balloons. If your group is larger than fifteen participants, determine how many colors of balloons you will need to create smaller groups of six to eight young people.

1. Give everyone an uninflated balloon and allow them to choose one paper from the bag or box. Caution them not to look at what is written on the paper, but to fold it to a size that will fit into the balloon. Then have them each put their paper into the balloon, inflate the balloon, and tie it off.

2. Explain that when you yell "popcorn!" the participants should each toss their balloon into the air. They do not have to keep track of their own balloon, but the object is to keep all the balloons in the air until you call time. When you call time, everyone should take a balloon.

When everyone is ready, yell "popcorn!" Allow the young people to bat the balloons around for about a minute, then call time. Be sure that each person has a balloon before you move on.

3. Tell the young people to gather in a group with others who have the same color balloon as they do. After they are in groups, they should determine the person who has the most consonants in his or her full name (first, middle, and last). When every group has named that person, explain that he or she will start the process. That person should burst his or her balloon, find the question, and read it to another person in the group. When that person answers the question, he or she should burst his or her balloon, find the question, and read it to someone else holding a balloon. The last person holding a balloon should direct the question to the person who started the process.

By the end of the game, everyone should have had a chance to burst their balloon, read a question, and answer one. If someone cannot answer a question, anyone else can jump in with the answer. The one who gives the correct answer is the next to burst a balloon.

ALTERNATIVE APPROACHES

◎ You can extend this activity by adding more questions and more balloons. It can go on as long as the young people have energy for it and your ears can take it!

◎ Save time by blowing up the balloons and inserting the questions before the session.

◎ If you have a small group, there is no need to purchase balloons of different colors. Use the same process for determining who breaks a balloon first and for getting through the group.

◎ If you have a large group but you are the only leader, have everyone burst their balloon and find the question at the same time. They can ask questions in turn. Anyone can answer, but be sure that the same people are not answering all the questions. If this starts to happen, impose a new rule that says only people who have not answered previously can answer. Ask those who have already answered to move to the side.

NOTES

Use the space below to jot notes and reminders for the next time you use this strategy.

What's the Meaning?
A Vocabulary Review Exercise

If you have a number of new terms that the young people need to know, this is a quick and active way to review. It is an ideal activity for any catechetical situation.

Suggested Time

5 to 10 minutes, or longer if needed

Group Size

This activity can be done with any size group.

Materials Needed

- ☼ a bag or box
- ☼ index cards, at least one per person
- ☼ markers
- ☼ masking tape (optional)

PROCEDURE

Preparation. Write each word or phrase that you want to review on a separate index card. Write the meaning or definition of each word or phrase on another index card. Be sure to have at least one pair of cards for every two people. You can, however, have a few more. Mix up the cards and put them in a box or bag.

1. Pass around the bag or box with the vocabulary cards and direct the teens each to take one card. If any cards remain in the bag or box, tape them to a wall or in another place where everyone can see them.

Tell the participants that when you give the signal, they should move around the room and find the person who has the match to their card. When they find that person, they should stand together and hold up their cards.

If you posted extra cards, make the young people aware that the match to their card may be hanging on the wall rather than in the hands of another person. If that is the case, they are to remove the posted card and hold both.

2. When everyone has found their match, ask the partners to take turns reading aloud what is on their cards as a way of reinforcing the lesson. If a person doesn't have a partner, she or he should read aloud both cards. If you sense that some teens are not comfortable reading in front of others, read the information yourself.

Collect the cards and repeat the process as many times as you can, being aware of the available time and the interest level of the young people.

ALTERNATIVE APPROACHES

◎ If you have many more vocabulary words than young people, divide the cards into two sets. Duplicate some of the more difficult words if you need to fill out the sets. Alternate sets when you repeat the activity.

◎ If you have a small group of teens, put the word cards in a bag or box and randomly place the definition cards on the floor. Have the teens take turns choosing a word card and then finding its definition.

NOTES

Use the space below to jot notes and reminders for the next time you use this strategy.

M&M Memory Starters
A Review Exercise

The participants use multicolored candies to review material. This is a good check-in activity for the beginning of classes or group meetings or any time you want to check on what the young people remember from your time together. You can use this activity several times in one session, changing the topics each time.

Suggested Time

The length of this activity depends on the number of people in the group and the number of rounds. Two rounds in a group of six people is likely to take about 10 minutes.

Group Size

This strategy works with any size group. However, if the group is larger than fifteen participants, you may want to form smaller groups.

Materials Needed

- ☼ a bag of multicolored candies, such as M&M's, Skittles, or jelly beans
- ☼ a bowl or bowls, one for each group
- ☼ newsprint and markers
- ☼ masking tape

PROCEDURE

Preparation. Empty a bag of multicolored candies into a bowl. If you have more than one group, you will need one bowl for each small group.

For each color of candy that appears in the bowl, you will need one review topic. Choose the topics based on the lesson you want to review. For example, if you are reviewing a lesson about Jesus' ministry, your categories might be these:

- red—describe one of Jesus' miracles
- yellow—retell one of Jesus' parables
- green—tell about one of Jesus' friends or family
- brown—tell something about the final week of Jesus' life
- orange—tell about something that happened after Jesus' Resurrection
- blue—tell about one of Jesus' Apostles

Be sure that your categories can elicit multiple answers from the same person in case someone happens to choose the same color of candy each round. Write the review topics on newsprint and indicate what color of candy is associated with each topic. Post the list.

1. Put the bowl of multicolored candies in the middle of the group. Point out the list you posted and explain that in turn each person will pick a candy from the bowl and talk about the topic associated with the color she or he chose. Note that no one should repeat information already given by someone else. If you think that the teens will be hesitant about being on the spot, assure them that they do not have to talk for any more than 30 seconds about the topic.

2. Ask for a volunteer to start, or choose a person at random. Hold the bowl for the first person above eye level while he or she randomly chooses a candy. Encourage the young people to listen carefully to one another and not get distracted.

Go through as many rounds of review topics as you have time for or the teens have interest in. Share the remainder of the candy with the group at snack time.

ALTERNATIVE APPROACHES

- Any object that comes in multiple forms can be used for this activity. For example, you could use animal crackers and associate each animal with a category. Use all the pieces of Alpha-Bits cereal that spell out the name of your group or church and associate each letter with a category. Or use non-food items such as marbles, Legos, or small squares of colored paper.
- You may want to end the activity by having everyone choose the category that they want to address.

NOTES

Use the space below to jot notes and reminders for the next time you use this strategy.

Deal Me In!

A Review Activity with Playing Cards

Playing cards provide the means by which the young people engage in reviewing material, using predetermined review topics. This activity works well for small groups and also as a periodic attention-getting activity during a retreat or a long session.

Suggested Time

A minimum of 5 minutes, depending on the size of the group and the number of rounds

Group Size

This strategy works with any size group, but if you have more than six people, you may want to form smaller groups and provide each group with a deck of cards.

Materials Needed

- ☼ newsprint and markers
- ☼ masking tape
- ☼ playing cards

PROCEDURE

Preparation. Choose four review topics, one for each of the four card suits. The topics should be directly related to the material you want to review. Be sure that you word the topics in a way that allows the same person to answer the question in a variety of ways, should someone be dealt the same suit more than once.

For example, if you are reviewing the Old Testament, your four topics might include these:

◎ hearts—something that happens in the Book of Genesis
◎ diamonds—something about one of the prophets
◎ clubs—recite any verse of a psalm
◎ spades—a historical fact that we know from the Old Testament

Draw the symbol for each suit—heart, diamond, club, and spade—down the left side of a sheet of newsprint. Next to each symbol write the review topic. Post the newsprint.

Shuffle the deck of cards, leaving in the two jokers. Deal a card to one person at a time. The person must respond to the corresponding review topic before you deal a card to the next person. That person cannot provide the same answer that someone else has given.

If you deal a joker to someone, the recipient may choose the topic. Go through as many rounds as you have time for.

ALTERNATIVE APPROACHES

◎ End the activity by letting everyone choose their own review topic.
◎ Consider starting your session with one of the playing card get-to-know-you activities in part C of *Community-Building Ideas for Ministry with Young Teens,* another volume in the HELP series.

NOTES

Use the space below to jot notes and reminders for the next time you use this strategy.

Part C
Prayer and Faith-Building Strategies

When it comes to prayer, young teens can be enigmatic. They like to move around, they like to be still. They like to make things with their hands, they like to imagine things in their mind's eye. They like to have fun, they like to be serious. In other words young teens bring their whole self to the experience of prayer.

This section contains ideas for prayer and reflection that address young teens' various needs. All the ideas engage the whole person in the process and practice of prayer.

Sacramental Journey

Pilgrimage, Prayer, and Discussion

OVERVIEW

This strategy invites the young people to pray with their feet. That is, they walk the path of a simulated journey through life and look at the sacraments as sources of strength along the way. It is an ideal activity to complement a course on sacraments or to make part of a catechetical retreat.

Suggested Time

This strategy takes a minimum of 2 hours, but it depends on where and how far apart you set up the stations.

Group Size

This strategy works best with groups of fewer than twenty participants. If your group is larger than twenty, assign the young people to small groups, each with its own adult leader.

Materials Needed

- ☼ extra notebooks or journals (optional)
- ☼ extra pens or pencils (optional)
- ☼ a backpack or something else to carry supplies
- ☼ a first aid kit

PROCEDURE

Preparation. Find a place that is conducive to a quiet walk. Choose a hiking trail at a nearby state park or a hike on the grounds of a local retreat center. Walk the trail and choose the seven spots where you will stop to reflect, discuss, and pray about each sacrament. Be sure to space the reflection spots far enough apart so that the teens have the feeling of a pilgrimage, but not so far apart that you have to rush to complete the activity in the amount of time you have.

Send a note to the young people before the event. Explain that they will be doing a lot of walking and that they should wear comfortable shoes and dress appropriately. Also tell them to bring along a bottle of water and a journal or notebook and something to write with. You may want to bring along extra notebooks and pens or pencils in case someone forgets.

1. When the young people gather, briefly introduce the concept of pilgrimage as part of our Catholic heritage. Make the following points in your own words:

The purpose of a pilgrimage is to enter into a special kind of prayer in a setting that has spiritual or religious significance.

Pilgrimages were especially popular in the days when transportation was quite primitive. People made pilgrimages by walking to sites that were important in the early history of the church. They prayed along the way.

Even today people make pilgrimages to holy places. Even though they do not walk the entire journey, pilgrims frequent places like the Holy Land, Rome, and Assisi. Pilgrimages are a special time of prayer, reflection, and worship.

Answer any questions the group may have about pilgrimages, then continue your presentation by focusing on the theme of the group's pilgrimage.

One of the ways we can begin to understand the seven sacraments is by viewing them as sources of strength throughout our life journey.

We receive some sacraments only once, but they continue to guide us throughout life. For example, we are baptized only once, but we are called to live out our baptismal promises to serve God and others every day. We are privileged to receive some sacraments—such as the Eucharist or Reconciliation—more often.

As we journey on foot, we will stop along the way to look at each of the sacraments and how each plays an important role in our life journey.

2. Invite the young people to walk the journey prayerfully, if not silently. At each sacrament stop, give a brief synopsis of the sacrament and answer any questions they may have. Form the teens into small groups of three or four people, and ask them to discuss the following questions:

What is this sacrament all about?

What challenge does it have for you in your life?

How can it be a source of strength in your everyday life?

3. Before leaving the sacrament stop, ask the teens to pause for some quiet time. Invite them to write a prayer inspired by the sacrament in their journal. If some teens are comfortable doing so, invite them to share their prayer before moving on to the next stop.

ALTERNATIVE APPROACHES

- Ask each person to choose one of the seven prayers they wrote on their walk. Collect the prayers and compile them into a small booklet of sacrament prayers to share with the entire group. You could also publish all the prayers that the teens wrote, grouping them by sacrament. With the teens' permission, give a copy to each person in the group, the parish staff, families of children and teenagers in sacramental preparation programs, and so forth.
- Part of the appeal of this activity is that it puts the young people in a quiet, natural environment that is conducive to prayer and reflection. However, with careful planning, it can also be done on the parish grounds and the nearby area. Include appropriate symbolic items, such as water, a stole, rings, oils, and choose appropriate sites for each stop, such as these:
  - *Baptism.* Baptismal font, gathering space, or vestibule
  - *Reconciliation.* In or in front of the Reconciliation room
  - *The Eucharist.* Altar, gathering space, kitchen
  - *Confirmation.* Baptismal font, local food pantry or soup kitchen, around the cabinet where the holy oils are kept
  - *Holy Orders.* Rectory, sacristy
  - *Marriage.* The home of a parish family
  - *Sacrament of Anointing of the Sick.* Sacristy (around the chrismatorium), on the grounds of a local hospital or nursing home
- Create a small journal specifically for this activity. Use scriptural quotes that can be associated with each sacrament, sacramental prayers from the book of rites, and symbols of each sacrament. Designate a page for the sacramental prayer in each section and leave room for other reflections.

NOTES

Use the space below to jot notes and reminders for the next time you use this strategy.

Doodle Prayers
A Creative Prayer Activity

This creative prayer activity invites the young teens to use their imagination and have fun transforming ordinary doodles into prayers. This activity can be used effectively in any setting.

Suggested Time

15 to 20 minutes

Group Size

This strategy works with any size group, but the project will be done in small groups of seven or eight people.

Special Considerations

This strategy works best if each small group works at a round table. However it can be done on the floor.

Materials Needed

- newsprint and markers
- pens or pencils
- large self-stick notes, 3-by-5 inches (optional)
- masking tape

PROCEDURE

Preparation. Recreate the following examples on newsprint. Post the sample, but keep it covered until directed to show it to the teens.

Dear God, help me to get through the ups and downs in my life.

Dear God, sometimes I feel like I am going around in circles.
Please help me to find my way.

Dear God, sometimes the mistakes I have made
make me feel like a giant knot inside. Please forgive me.

1. Form the participants into small groups of seven or eight people. Another volume in the HELP series, *Community-Building Ideas for Ministry with Young Teens,* includes creative strategies for forming small groups.

Give each small group a sheet of newsprint and some markers. Invite the teens to begin doodling on the newsprint. They can use any colors they choose, but their doodles must be small enough so that each person in the group has a chance to create at least two examples. Challenge the groups to cover the paper with doodles.

2. After the paper has been covered, invite the young people to think of prayers to match some of the doodles on their sheet. They can write a prayer that matches one of their own doodles or one that someone else created. Several people can use the same doodle because their prayer may be different.

Tell the groups that each person is to create prayers for at least two of the doodles on the newsprint. The prayers can be as short as one sentence or as long as a paragraph. Each prayer should be written somewhere around the doodle that it accompanies. (If you prefer, give each person two large self-stick notes and tell them to write a prayer on each note. When it is time to share their prayers, they are to attach the notes beside the doodles.)

Display the samples that you created before the session to give the young people an idea of the type of prayer you are looking for.

3. Give the young teens time to create their prayers. Then invite them to read aloud their prayer(s) to the others in their small group. If time permits, you may invite volunteers to share some of their examples with the large group.

4. Close by asking the young people what they learned from this activity. Challenge them to use their imagination to find prayer in the ordinary and everywhere, and remind them that prayer can be fun!

(This strategy is taken from *Pathways to Praying with Teens,* by Maryann Hakowski, pp. 88–89.)

ALTERNATIVE APPROACHES

◎ Instead of giving each group a separate sheet of paper, cover the walls of your meeting space with large butcher paper and allow the young people to create their doodle prayers all over the room. Display the finished product in a gathering space at the parish.

◎ Invite the young teens to doodle on the paper at the start of the session, but save the sharing of the prayers until the closing prayer at the end of the session.

◎ Give each person two index cards for drawing their doodles and two cards for writing prayers. When everyone has doodled, gather the cards, shuffle them, and distribute them randomly. Direct the teens to write a prayer for each doodle they received on a separate card. After they share their prayers, create a prayer collage by arranging the prayers with their respective doodles in a pattern around your youth room or classroom.

NOTES

Use the space below to jot notes and reminders for the next time you use this strategy.

Prayer Box

Creating a Portable Sacred Space

OVERVIEW

This activity helps the young people understand that they can create their own sacred space for prayer wherever they are. It also helps them understand how symbols can help us focus our prayer.

Suggested Time

This activity can take 60 minutes over two sessions or be done over several weeks. It depends on how many of the items the teens actually make and how much decorating they do.

Group Size

The strategy can be done with any size group as long as enough adult supervision is available.

Special Considerations

This activity can be simple or highly elaborate. As the process is outlined in this plan, it will take a medium amount of time to complete. In most cases both simpler and more elaborate options are provided.

Materials Needed

- ☼ boxes, one for each person
- ☼ old magazines, used greeting cards, and other sources of photos and words
- ☼ fabric, sequins, beads, Styrofoam, and other sources of textured items
- ☼ glue, scissors, markers, and other craft supplies
- ☼ Mod Podge, slightly diluted white glue, or spray varnish (optional)
- ☼ paintbrushes (optional)
- ☼ a Bible
- ☼ a rosary
- ☼ votive candles, one for each person
- ☼ baby food jars, one for each person
- ☼ a journal
- ☼ inexpensive notebooks, one for each person
- ☼ craft sticks and toothpicks for making crosses
- ☼ small plastic bottles, one for each person

PROCEDURE

Preparation. Purchase or find a box with a lid for each person. The box should be larger than a shoe box, but small enough to be easily carried around. Ideally the box should be approximately 9-by-12 inches with a depth of 5 to 7 inches, similar to boxes that business envelopes come in. If cardboard boxes are not available, purchase a plastic storage box for each person.

Decide how simple or how elaborate you want this project to be. Consider your available time, supplies, and the usual level of enthusiasm of the young people for such projects. Make a plan for how you will facilitate the project over one or several sessions.

Using procedure steps 2 and 3 below, create and fill your own box to show the young people what the final product will be like. Make your box as elaborate as your choice of options dictates.

1. Introduce the activity by making the following comments in your own words:

> Prayer can happen anytime, anyplace, and in any manner. All one really needs is a spirit that is attentive to the presence of God.
>
> Many things can help our spirit be more attentive. Candles, a Bible, a cross, a rosary, and many other religious items remind us that God is present.

Announce that each person will create his or her own portable prayer space containing a number of prayerful items gathered in one box. This box will be transformed into something worthy of the treasure that it holds.

Display the box that you created before the session. Give the young people a chance to look it over carefully. You may need to explain some of the things you put on the box.

2. Give each person a box. Make a variety of old magazines, used greeting cards, fabric, sequins, beads, Styrofoam, glue, scissors, markers, and other craft supplies available. Allow enough time for the young people to get as creative as they want to be in decorating their own box. You might want to set some guidelines, depending on the time you have allotted for the completion of this activity. For example, if you are doing it over several weeks, you might direct the teens to decorate every inch of the cover and sides. If you have little time, suggest that they cut the letters of their name out of paper and put them on top of the box, then add five pictures that remind them of God's presence.

When the teens are finished with their boxes, you may want to have them paint a thin coat of Mod Podge, slightly diluted white glue, or spray a light coat of varnish on the box. This will be especially helpful if the boxes are elaborately decorated.

3. While the boxes are drying, explain what will go on the inside of the box. Use your own box as a sample. The following items can make up the contents of the box:

◎ *A Bible.* Invite the young people to bring their Bible to the next session to place in the box. Note that the Scriptures are an important part of how Catholics pray—both as a community and as individuals.

　　Extended option. During a future session, have the young people create Bible bookmarks for themselves or one another.

◎ *A rosary.* Show the rosary that you included in your own box. Explain that reciting the rosary is a traditional Catholic prayer. If they are unfamiliar with the rosary, take the time to teach the basics to them. Ask them to bring a rosary from home to the next class. They should also find out the family history of their rosary so that they can tell the rest of the group. Was it their grandmother's rosary? Did their dad use the rosary for his first Communion?

　　Simple option. Purchase inexpensive rosaries for each young person at a religious supply store.

　　Extended option. Make beads, crosses, and cord available to the young people and allow them to create their own rosary. Or provide each person with a length of cord and knot the cord to form beads at appropriate places.

◎ *A candle.* Show your candle to the young people and explain the significance of the candle to you. Invite the young people to share their thoughts on why we light candles when we pray. For example, candles burn during Mass and possibly during prayer time in your sessions. It is one way we remind ourselves of the light of Christ always present with us and within us.

Give each person a small baby food jar and a votive candle. Lead the young people through the candleholder-making activity in part A of this book, "The Light of Christ."

Simple option. Give each person a vigil candle in a holder or a small pillar candle.

Extended option. Purchase candle-making kits at a local craft supply store. Have the young people make their own candles for the jar, or use empty cans or orange juice containers as a mold for pillar candles.

◎ *A journal.* Show the young people your journal. If you feel comfortable doing so, read an excerpt from it. Talk about how keeping a journal is one way people communicate with God.

Give each young person an inexpensive notebook. The bound black-and-white composition books are best because they tend to have sturdy covers. Allow time for the young people to personalize their book with the available supplies.

Simple option. Do not personalize the books other than with the young person's name. Or tell them to decorate their cover at home.

Extended option. Allow the young people to create their own journal with a three-ring binder, colored and decorated papers as well as plain paper, their favorite photographs, and so forth.

◎ *A cross or crucifix.* Point out that the cross or crucifix is a symbol of the great sacrifice Jesus made for us. The basis of our faith is the death and Resurrection of Jesus. Crosses decorate our homes, classrooms, churches, clothing, ears, and so forth. Provide craft sticks and toothpicks, and allow each young person to create his or her own cross.

Simple option. Purchase an inexpensive cross for each person.

Extended option. In addition to craft sticks, provide clothespins, beads, leather cord, twigs, yarn, and so forth, and invite the young people to create a cross in their own style and expression.

◎ *Holy water.* Remind the teens that water is used at Baptism and is one of the first symbols of the Catholic faith. Every time we bless ourselves with holy water, we are reminded of our baptismal call to serve God and others.

Purchase a small plastic bottle for each person. Such bottles can be found among the travel items at any discount store. As a group, walk to the holy water dispenser in the church and fill the bottles.

Simple option. Purchase small bottles of holy water at a religious goods store.

Extended option. Have each person bring in at least one small empty bottle from vanilla extract, perfume, or a travel-size toiletry. Clean the bottles, fill them, and have a priest bless the water.

4. At this or a future session, add the prayer items to the box. Invite the young people to take their box home and use it during their prayer time every day. In good weather they might take it outside on the porch or to a park. Also, different places in the house will give them a different perspective of God.

Invite them to add their own symbols to their box over the next few weeks, such as photos of people they love, elements of nature, colored cloth, and any other symbols that speak to them.

◎ Incorporate the prayer box into periodic classes, sessions, and retreats. Inform the young people when they will need to bring their prayer box. Give them time to share about the things they have added to the box or some significant prayer times.

◎ When the boxes are finally completed and before the young people take them home, conduct a blessing service, blessing both the contents and the owner of each box.

Use the space below to jot notes and reminders for the next time you use this strategy.

Prayer Pillows
A Prayer Craft Project

This craft activity challenges the young people to think about and better understand the Reign of God. It also invites them to consider what is really valuable in their life. The pillow becomes a tangible reminder of how they should live each day as if the Reign of God were already fulfilled on earth.

Suggested Time

60 to 120 minutes

Group Size

This strategy can be done with any size group as long as ample supervision is available and you have access to enough sewing machines.

Special Considerations

The success of this strategy depends to a great extent on your access to and knowledge of a sewing machine. Ideally this strategy should be done in a location with ready access to machines.

Materials Needed

- ☼ a candle and matches
- ☼ a Bible

- newsprint and markers
- pieces of corduroy fabric, about 14 inches square, one for each person
- pieces of white cotton fabric, about 14 inches square, one for each person
- fabric paints or colorful permanent markers
- pencils
- small pieces of paper, several for each person
- cotton batting or other pillow-filling materials

PROCEDURE

Preparation. Begin making the pillows by putting a piece of cotton and a piece of corduroy together (be sure the outside surface of the corduroy faces in) and sewing together three sides. Then turn the pillow inside out so the outside surface of the corduroy faces out.

You may want to complete one pillow as a sample.

1. Light a candle in your meeting space. Recruit two people to each read aloud one of the following Scripture passages:
- Matt. 13:44–46
- Matt. 6:19–21

After the readings allow silence to linger while the teens reflect on what they have heard. Then invite them to take turns completing the following phrase aloud:

For me, the Reign of God is . . .

Whenever someone completes the statement, repeat the sentence-starter so that someone else can complete it.

After all who want to add their thought have had a chance to do so, close the prayer time and review what people said the Reign of God is for them. If many people responded, list their ideas on newsprint.

2. Give each person a semi-completed pillow. Make markers or fabric paints available for the whole group. Tell the teens to write the phrase "The Reign of God is . . ." on the white part of the pillow and to fill in the rest of the white material with words and phrases to express their answers.

3. Give each person a pencil and several small slips of paper and ask them to consider the treasures in their life. Remind them to focus on nonmaterial treasures. Ask questions like the following:

What do you really value?

What is really important in your life?

Who or what could you not imagine life without?

If they are having trouble coming up with ideas, give examples, such as their health, their parents, freedom, the dog, the ability to sing, and so forth. Encourage the teens to be as honest as possible and to write as many treasures as they can think of. Assure them that no one will see these treasures.

4. Make the pillow-stuffing material available and tell the young people to mix their treasures with pillow-stuffing materials and stuff their pillow. If possible, have a sewing machine ready to close up the open end of the pillows.

5. Encourage the young people to take their pillow home to rest on when they pray. Tell them to use the pillow as a reminder to thank God in prayer for their treasures and to continue to live as if the Reign of God were the way of the world.
Conclude the activity by reading aloud Matt. 11:28–30.

ALTERNATIVE APPROACHES

- If you do not have access to a sewing machine, ask for volunteers from the parish to bring their portable machines and help out for the evening.
- Ask the members of the parish quilting club to prepare the pillows by sewing three sides by hand. They may even be willing to come to your session and complete the process by hand. This would make a valuable connection between the teens and other members of the parish.
- Use the same process, but focus the activity on thanksgiving. The pillows then would contain prayers of things the teens are grateful for.

NOTES

Use the space below to jot notes and reminders for the next time you use this strategy.

Prayer with Empty Pockets

A Spontaneous Prayer Exercise

OVERVIEW

This prayer technique can be done spontaneously during a class, a retreat, or a youth group meeting. Besides being quick and easy, it shows the young people that prayer can be found anywhere and in anything. It also teaches in a fun way how symbols can be used in prayer.

Suggested Time

10 to 20 minutes

Group Size

This strategy works best with fifteen or fewer teens. If you have more than fifteen teens, form them into small groups of eight to ten.

PROCEDURE

1. Gather the young people in a circle and ask them each to place two objects in the center of the circle. The objects should be things they have with them in a pocket, purse, or backpack, like a comb, a family photo, a pack of gum, a key chain, a pen, a tissue, or a book.

2. Tell the young people to take a few minutes to look at all the objects in the center and think of a prayer that might be inspired by one of the objects. They may use any object in the circle for prayer, not just the ones they added. You might want to give examples such as the following:

◎ *Comb.* Dear God, please help me straighten out the things that tangle up my life.
◎ *Family picture.* Dear God, please watch over those that I love so much.

3. Give everyone a chance to share at least one prayer. They may take the object and hold it through their prayer, but then the object should be returned to the circle. Several people may choose the same object for prayer because each person's prayer will be different.

If time permits, you may allow each person to share a second prayer.

4. Close by encouraging the teens to look for opportunities for prayer all around them every day. Emphasize that prayer is not confined to just what we think of as religious symbols. Prayer can be found in all sorts of surprising places if we open our eyes and use our imagination.

ALTERNATIVE APPROACHES

◎ If your meeting space is filled with a variety of objects and decorated with a variety of things, you might ask the young people to choose anything they see in the room and use that symbol as a starting point for prayer.

◎ If you suspect that the young people will not have enough of a variety of objects, put together a box of common office supplies, household objects, and so forth.

◎ Before they come to the session, ask the teens to bring one or two of their favorite things from their room at home. When they arrive, use these objects as the basis for prayer.

NOTES

Use the space below to jot notes and reminders for the next time you use this strategy.

Three Questions

An Exercise in Shared Prayer

OVERVIEW

This activity introduces the young people to shared prayer and encourages them to pray from their own cares, concerns, and questions. It gives teens the option of praying aloud or in silence, being assured of the support of the gathered community either way.

Suggested Time

About 30 minutes

Group Size

This strategy works best with groups of less than thirty people

Special Considerations

Many young teens are self-conscious about praying aloud in a group. Everyone should be encouraged to pray aloud, but some young teens may choose another form of expression that they are more comfortable with. You will probably find that the longer your group is together, the more comfortable they will become with sharing prayer aloud.

Materials Needed

- ☼ index cards in three colors, one of each color per person plus a few extras
- ☼ markers
- ☼ pencils or pens
- ☼ a pillar candle and matches
- ☼ a tape or CD player, and a recording of reflective music (optional)
- ☼ a basket

PROCEDURE

Preparation. Write the three following words and their corresponding explanations, each on a different color index card:

- ◎ *Care.* What or who do I care about?
- ◎ *Concern.* What or who am I concerned about?
- ◎ *Question.* What or who do I have questions about?

1. Gather the young people in a circle and place the three stacks of index cards in the center. Each stack should be a different color. Near each stack, place the corresponding explanation card that you prepared before the session. Give each young person a pen or pencil.

Light the candle before you start your comments. Also you may want to play reflective music during this time if it is available.

2. Introduce this activity by noting that people can start a conversation with God in many different ways. The name for that conversation is prayer. Then explain the process as follows:

> In the center of the group are three stacks of cards. Each stack represents a different question. The care cards ask, "What or who do I care about?" The concern cards ask, "What or who am I concerned about?" The question cards ask, "What or who do I have questions about?"

> Decide which card represents something or someone you want to bring to God. Then come forward quietly, take a card back to your place, and write a prayer on the card. Please remain quiet so that other people can think and write.

> If you want to write more than one prayer, you are welcome to do so.

> Allow a few minutes for the teens to take their cards and write their prayer.

3. After all the young people are finished, explain that you will pass a basket around the circle. Invite the young people to read one prayer aloud and then put their card or cards in the basket. If someone is uncomfortable sharing their prayer aloud, that person should simply place his or her card in the basket and hold the basket for a time of quiet prayer.

Close by encouraging the young people to continue bringing their cares, concerns, and questions to God in prayer. Read Matt. 7:7–11 to conclude your prayer time.

ALTERNATIVE APPROACHES

◎ Instead of having the young people read their own prayer, pass the basket and collect all the prayers. Mix them up. Redistribute the prayers randomly and have the teens read them aloud. This process adds an element of anonymity that may make it easier for some people.

◎ If the young people enjoy this prayer, you may want to do it again. Instead of the three words used in this session plan, use three different words, such as *feel, worry, celebrate, wonder, thanksgiving, help.*

◎ If you do the prayer again, ask the young people which words and questions they want to focus on. Decide on three words and the questions they represent. It will take a little longer, but the young people may feel more ownership of the process.

NOTES

Use the space below to jot notes and reminders for the next time you use this strategy.

Communication Golf

A Lesson on Obstacles to Communication

In this activity the young people create a miniature golf course to simulate the difficulties of communicating well with others. The teens identify obstacles, have fun creating the course, and then offer solutions to the problems. This is an ideal activity for a course or retreat on friendship or communication.

Suggested Time

120 to 180 minutes

Group Size

The activity works best with a group larger than twenty-five people. Form the young people into smaller work groups of five or six people each.

Special Considerations

A gym or large open room is needed for this activity. Clear the space, with the exception of a few tables. Cover the tables with assorted craft and construction supplies.

Materials Needed

- ☼ newsprint and markers
- ☼ assorted supplies, such as various sizes of cardboard boxes, paper cups, coffee filters, wooden dowels or sticks, wrapping tape or duct tape, newsprint, pieces of PVC pipe, heavy construction paper, small toys, and any other odds and ends
- ☼ assorted art supplies
- ☼ Ping-Pong balls, one per person
- ☼ golf putters or dowels, duct tape, and Styrofoam blocks for making home-made putters

PROCEDURE

1. Introduce the activity by making the point that communication is an exchange of information between two or more people. It can happen with words or with actions and attitudes. People want to communicate effectively, but many things stand in the way. Ask the teens to call out things that might stand in the way of good communication between two people. List their answers on newsprint. The list may include some of the following: judgment, hostility, preoccupation, lack of respect, inattention, lack of focus, put-downs, defensiveness, narrow opinions, vagueness, silliness, avoidance of the issue, or anger. Encourage everyone to join in the brainstorming session.

2. Have the young people form smaller groups of five or six people each. You may want to consult another volume in the HELP series, *Community-Building Ideas for Ministry with Young Teens,* for ideas for forming small groups in a nonthreatening and creative way.

Announce that each small group will create its own "obstacle to communication" in the form of a miniature golf course hole. Point out the available supplies, and encourage the groups to be as creative as possible.

The groups should label their golf course holes with names hinting at the obstacle to communication they represent. For example, one hole could start on top of a cardboard box with a downward track. It could be named the "Putt-down." The course could then lead into a box opening that represents a circus tent and is named "Silly city." The ball might start toward the next hole through a narrow PVC pipe called "Narrow arrow," then take a number of sharp curves named "Hocus focus" before dropping into the hole.

3. As they finish their creations, allow the groups to work together to set up the course. They may want to make flags or other markers for the holes or otherwise decorate the course.

4. Provide Ping-Pong balls and putters (or have the young people make their own putters using dowels, duct tape, and Styrofoam blocks), and invite the teens to play the course. Challenge them to guess the obstacle of communication each hole represents before the creators announce the name of the hole.

After each hole is played, ask the young people to offer some ideas for overcoming that particular obstacle of communication before playing through to the next hole.

ALTERNATIVE APPROACHES

◎ If you do not have a large open area available to you, change this exercise into a mini-miniature golf course by using marbles, paper towel tubes, Legos, and small gift boxes.

◎ If the people in your group are on the younger end of the young adolescent spectrum, you may want to assign a communication obstacle to each group and ask them to figure out a way to represent it as a golf hole. Doing this will speed up the process slightly by eliminating one group decision. They can put all their creative energies into thinking of ways to make it happen.

NOTES

Use the space below to jot notes and reminders for the next time you use this strategy.

Balloon Relay Race

A Lesson in Community and Perseverance

The young teens become familiar with two words seen frequently in the Bible: *community* and *perseverance.*

Suggested Time

40 to 60 minutes

Group Size

This strategy works best with five to twenty-five young people.

Materials Needed

- ☼ masking tape
- ☼ party balloons, 8 to 10 inches in diameter, one per person
- ☼ a reward or treat for each person (optional)
- ☼ Bibles, one per person
- ☼ newsprint and markers
- ☼ a pillar candle and matches
- ☼ a tape or CD player, and a recording of reflective music (optional)

PROCEDURE

Preparation. Use masking tape to designate a starting line and a finish line. The lines should be a minimum of 25 feet apart, but can be as long as 40 feet apart. They should be long enough to accommodate five teams.

Print the following scriptural citations on newsprint:

- Acts 2:43–47
- Acts 14:21–28
- Luke 11:5–13
- 1 Cor. 9:24–27

1. Divide the group into teams of no more than five people. You may want to consult another volume in the HELP series, *Community-Building Ideas for Ministry with Young Teens,* for creative, objective, and nonthreatening ways to form small groups. If some teams have fewer participants, ask the first person on those teams to take a second turn at the end of the line.

2. Give each person a balloon and let her or him practice blowing it up and letting the air out. Some young teens may need a little help getting their balloon started.

Explain that, in turn, each person is to blow up his or her balloon and let it go, aiming it in the direction of the finish line. If the person's balloon does not go over the line, he or she should move to the spot where it landed and repeat the process until the balloon crosses the line. When that happens the next person in line can begin blowing his or her balloon. Others on the team should act as cheerleaders, shouting their support and encouragement.

The goal is to have all team members cross the finish line with their balloon. The team to do so first wins. You may want to award small prizes or treats to the winning team.

3. Explain briefly the following points in your own words:

Two concepts frequently found in the Scriptures are community and perseverance. Community means working together for the common good, supporting one another, and encouraging one another. The New Testament, particularly the Acts of the Apostles and the letters to the early church, are full of references to the experience of community.

Perseverance means keeping at something until it is finished. It means that we must keep on trying to reach our goals, despite setbacks, frustration, lack of progress, and other obstacles. The Scriptures call people to perseverance in their prayer life, community life, and their spiritual growth.

Point out that both community and perseverance were evident during the balloon game. Ask the young people to give examples of each characteristic they saw evidenced during the game. Supplement their examples with your own.

4. Distribute Bibles. Read each of the following scriptural passages aloud—or recruit a young person to do so—and lead the group in a discussion around the accompanying questions:

◎ *Acts 2:43–47*
   ◎ Which words in the passage describe community?
   ◎ How is the community described in the passage similar to the community gathered here?
   ◎ How is the community described in the passage similar to your family community?
   ◎ How is the community described in the passage similar to your parish community?

◎ *Luke 11:5–13*
   ◎ When has someone bugged you or nagged you to do something for them?
   ◎ Do you ever feel like you are nagging God?
   ◎ Do you ever feel like God is nagging you?

5. Gather the group in a circle. Light a candle and place it in the middle of the group. If you have reflective music available, begin playing it at this time. After a few moments of silence, make the following comments in your own words:

Being part of a community is essential to healthy growth as human beings. Most people belong to several communities.

We learn to be our best self in our communities. We learn how to be persistent in getting what we need. We learn to hone our skills and engage in healthy competition with others, with the assurance that we will remain a valued part of the community. This is one element of living life as a Christian.

Saint Paul says that living the Christian life is like running a race. A Christian must persevere much like a runner. We have to try and try again if we are going to ever be really good at following in Jesus' footsteps.

6. Explain that the prayer will focus on the image of the Christian life as a race. Invite the young people to complete the following sentence-starter silently and then aloud if they wish to do so. They can complete the sentence with one word or a series of phrases—whichever feels most comfortable to them.

The race I need help with most right now is . . .

After everyone who wants to speak has had a chance to do so, close the session by reading 1 Cor. 9:24–27.

ALTERNATIVE APPROACHES

- To add further challenge to the balloon relay, use tape to plot out a lane for each team that is about 4 feet wide. When released the balloon must land in the lane. If not, the blower tries again from the same spot.
- After the relay tell the young people to blow up their balloon and tie it off. On the count of three, have everyone try to burst their balloon. Before moving on, tell the participants to pick up every piece of balloon within a 10-foot radius of where they are standing and dispose of the pieces. Refer to this activity when talking about the idea of a community of people working together.
- Instead of discussing both scriptural passages with the whole group, divide the group in half and have each smaller group discuss one passage, then share the results with the full group.
- If you are doing this activity as part of a longer retreat, you may want to add other team-building activities to highlight the concepts of community and perseverance. *Community-Building Ideas for Ministry with Young Teens* has many suggestions for such activities.

NOTES

Use the space below to jot notes and reminders for the next time you use this strategy.

A Gift from Jesus

A Guided Reflection with Clay

This strategy engages the young teens in two activities that most people their age find particularly appealing: guided meditation and working with clay to create something out of nothing. It is an ideal activity for an extended session or a retreat on the theme of grace or giftedness.

Suggested Time

30 to 45 minutes

Group Size

This strategy works best with groups of less than thirty people.

Materials Needed

- ☼ a Bible
- ☼ blank sheets of paper, one for each person
- ☼ Sculpty or another brand of modeling clay
- ☼ plastic sandwich bags
- ☼ a tape or CD player, and a recording of reflective music (optional)

PROCEDURE

Preparation. Prepare a small bag of modeling clay for each young person.

1. Begin the session by reading aloud the story of Zacchaeus in Luke 19:1–10. Encourage the young people to listen carefully to the details. After you read the story, lead a discussion around the following questions:

What did Zacchaeus do for a living?

What was his physical stature like?

How did he get to see Jesus?

What did Jesus say to Zacchaeus?

Why were people upset with Jesus?

What gift did Jesus bring to Zacchaeus that day?

The teens will likely be stumped by the last question, because the story does not say anything about Jesus bringing a gift. Point out that the result of Jesus' visit was that Zacchaeus repented for the things he did wrong and became a disciple. The gift that Jesus gave to Zacchaeus that day was the challenge to allow God into his home and his heart. Because Zacchaeus accepted the challenge, his life was changed.

2. Give each young person a piece of paper. Announce that they will have a chance to enter into a story similar to the story of Zacchaeus. Tell the young people to move to a place in the room where they can be comfortable and alone with their thoughts. Encourage them to lie down if they want to, but to stay far enough away from other people so that they do not get distracted or distract others.

You may want to begin playing reflective music if it is available. Begin the guided meditation with a relaxation process. One way to do this is to ask the young people to tighten and release various muscle groups, starting with their toes and ending with their upper extremities. Use a soothing tone of voice and style of speech and give the young people several seconds between each directive so that they do not feel rushed.

When they are quiet and relaxed, begin the following meditation. Pause for a few seconds at each set of ellipses.

In your mind's eye, imagine yourself walking toward home on a busy street. It's a bright, beautiful day. The air is light and clean, with just a hint of a breeze. . . . What do you see around you? . . . You've walked this street before many times, but it seems to be especially busy today for some reason. As you make your way toward home, you notice a huge crowd up ahead. You stand back and look at all the people. . . . Do you recognize anyone? . . .

As you get closer, you hear a lot of commotion. What do you hear? . . . You ask someone what is going on. The person tells you that someone famous is in town. He forgot the person's name, though. No one knew he was coming. He just showed up today. Everyone is trying to get a glimpse of this person, including you. . . . You move around the crowd, but you can't quite see who's in the middle. . . . You ask someone else, and that person tells you that Jesus came to town this morning. No one expected him. He just showed up. Now you *really* want to get a glimpse of him.

You notice a fence nearby. You know that if you can climb to the top of the fence, you can see into the middle of the crowd. So you make your way toward the fence and climb. . . . Finally you are at a height where you can see Jesus. What does he look like? . . . Does he look like you expected him to look? . . . What is he wearing? . . . Who is with him? . . . Just as you are getting comfortable on your perch, Jesus looks up—straight at you. He calls you by name and tells you that he's been waiting for you. He tells you to get off the fence and come to him. Do it now, the people will let you through. . . .

Now you're face-to-face with Jesus. How tall is he compared to you? . . . He calls you by name . . . and says to you, "I'm coming to your house for dinner tonight. And I need to stay there for the night too. Is that okay?" . . . What do you say to him? . . . How do you feel about the evening ahead? . . . You rush home and tell your family what happened. What happens next? . . .

Jesus arrives about three hours later. You answer the door and let him in. Dinner is not quite ready yet, so you talk with him alone for a while. He asks how you've been doing—really. Tell him. . . . Then he says to you, "I have a gift for you. It's just what you need right now!" Since you were the one who let him in, you know that he didn't bring a bag or a box. What gift could Jesus be giving you that is *exactly* what you need right now? . . .

3. While the young people are still meditating, quietly place a bag of modeling clay at their side. Try not to disturb their thoughts.

Gently and gradually bring the young people back from their meditation. Call them to this place and time. Ask them to open their eyes slowly and sit up, but to remain quiet. Call their attention to the bag of clay at their side, and encourage them to continue their meditation by molding the clay into something that represents the gift that Jesus gave them in their meditation. If they need an example, use one of the following:

If, like Zacchaeus, the gift was the challenge to be a follower of Jesus, they might mold their clay into a pair of sandals or a shoe.

If the gift was the courage to stand up for something they believe in, they might mold their clay into a podium or microphone.

If the gift was a willingness to forgive someone, they might mold their clay into an open door.

Allow about 10 minutes for the young people to make their clay creations. Tell them to place their completed clay creation on their piece of paper. If you have been doing so, continue playing reflective music to maintain the meditative mood.

4. Gather the young people in a circle. Allow a few minutes for them to examine one another's work. Invite those who want to do so to explain their clay creation to the group and what gift it represents.

Close the session by reading aloud Eph. 2:7–10.

ALTERNATIVE APPROACHES

◎ Instead of reading the story of Zacchaeus, ask a few young people to dramatize it. Contact them well before the session so that they have time to prepare. Provide props, costumes, and so forth.

◎ If you do not have the resources to purchase clay, many children's craft books have recipes for making clay out of common baking items.

◎ Instead of clay give each person a sheet of construction paper and ask them to rip the paper into a symbol of the gift Jesus gave them. This method is noisier and less meditative, but less costly and accomplishes the same purpose.

NOTES

Use the space below to jot notes and reminders for the next time you use this strategy.

Broken Pots

A Lesson in Piecing Together a History

The young people will piece together a broken pot to simulate their faith story. Each piece represents a particular aspect of their history: family, parish, prayer, youth camp, and so forth. This is a good activity for sacramental preparation classes, retreats, or sessions on religious heritage and tradition.

Suggested Time

About 30 minutes

Group Size

This strategy works best with groups of twenty or fewer.

Materials Needed

- ☼ clay pots, one for each person
- ☼ plastic zipper bags, one for each person
- ☼ permanent markers, one for each person
- ☼ tacky glue, pottery glue, or duct tape
- ☼ a pillar candle and matches, a colorful cloth, a cross, and other items for a prayer space
- ☼ a tape or CD player, and a recording of reflective music (optional)

PROCEDURE

Preparation. Purchase an inexpensive clay pot for each person. Break each pot into several pieces, keeping in mind that the pot must be reassembled. Remove three or four pieces and set them aside. Put the remaining pieces in a plastic zipper bag. Make one bag for each person.

You may want to break a pot for yourself and put it back together to show as an example.

1. Introduce this activity by reminding the young people that each of us brings a lifetime of experiences to this time and place. We each have a story to tell about the people and experiences that brought us to this point in our faith journey.

2. Give each young person a bag with the pieces of a pot and a permanent marker. Comment that by the end of our life we will be whole pots, but right now, we are putting all the pieces together. Each piece represents one part of our faith journey. Tell them to write on the outside of each piece the experiences or people that have been important in their own journey. For example, they might write "grandmother" on one piece, "Camp Victory when I was ten" on another, "family traditions," "Sunday Mass," "the beach in the morning," or any number of other things that have contributed significantly to getting them to this point. Allow 5 to 10 minutes for this part of the exercise.

3. Make available pottery glue, tacky glue, or duct tape. Tell them to put their pot back together. If they are using duct tape, tell them to cut the pieces small so that they do not cover up their writing or to put the tape on the inside of the pot.

While they are putting their pots back together, set up a prayer space with a candle, a colored cloth, and other decorative items. Also include in the space the pieces of clay that you set aside. If you have reflective music available, set up the tape or CD player.

4. When everyone has done the best job they can of putting their pot back together, gather the teens around the prayer space. By now they all will have discovered that several pieces are missing. Point out the extra pieces in the prayer space. Reiterate the remarks you made at the beginning of the session:

By the end of our life we will be whole pots, but right now we are putting all the pieces together. Because we are still on the journey, some pieces have yet to be uncovered.

Ask the young people the following questions:

What will you need in the future to build your relationship with God?

What experiences and people do you anticipate coming into your life that will reveal more of God to you?

In answering the first question, they might say things like more prayer or a stronger desire to know God. Their responses to the second question might be lifelong friendships, a marriage partner, deep sadness, or joy.

Close the discussion by commenting that every day of the rest of our life will bring opportunities to build our relationship with God. And if we take those opportunities, we move closer to adding another piece of the pot, another step toward completeness.

5. Light the candle. Invite the young people to a moment of silence, then read the following adaptation of Sir. 33:13:

Like clay in the hands of the potter, to be molded according to the potter's wishes, so are human beings in the hands of their Maker, to be given whatever the Maker knows is right.

Invite the young people one by one to bring their pot to the prayer space and lay it around the candle. As they do so, say these words from the Book of Isaiah: "God, you are the potter, we are the clay." Everyone should respond "We are the work of your hands" (adapted from Isa. 64:8).

Close with a group recitation of the traditional prayer known as the Glory Be.

ALTERNATIVE APPROACHES

◎ If you cannot purchase clay pots for everyone, an alternative might be to use large disposable cups and cut them up, or appropriate pictures from magazines. The cup or picture, like the pot, represents a person. Again, leave several pieces out.

◎ If your group is small, ask the teens to bring their markers to the prayer space. Distribute the leftover pieces of pots. Have the young people write their answers to the two questions on the pieces. Place them around the candle during the closing prayer.

◎ If you have a large group, have three or four people bring their pots to the central prayer space at the same time. Pause in between each group to re-establish the mood of reverence.

NOTES

Use the space below to jot notes and reminders for the next time you use this strategy.

God Can

An Exercise in Letting Go

In this activity the young people create a "God can," that is, a receptacle for the problems they face that they cannot seem to fix on their own. The can becomes a visual reminder of the need to let go of our difficulties and hand them over to God. This activity can be used in any setting and with any group.

Suggested Time

About 20 minutes

Group Size

This strategy can be done with any size group.

Materials Needed

- ☼ empty, clean soft drink cans, one for each person
- ☼ 8½-by-11-inch plain white paper, one sheet for each person
- ☼ pencils
- ☼ markers
- ☼ a variety of craft supplies, such as used magazines, stickers, fabric, glue sticks, and so forth
- ☼ cellophane tape, one roll for every three or four people
- ☼ 1½-by-4-inch pieces of plain paper, about three or four for every person

PROCEDURE

1. Ask the young people to think about a time when they worried about something that they really could not do anything about. For some it may have been an athletic event, for others, a family problem or a social event. If anyone wants to share the incident with the group, invite them to do so. Then lead a discussion around the following questions:

What do you do when you're worried about someone or something?

Does worrying about something help the problem? Why or why not?

What are some positive steps a person could take to lessen the worry in his or her life?

Be sure that the answers to the last question include giving one's worries to God. Conclude the first part of this activity by reading Matt. 6:25–26.

2. Give each young person an empty soft drink can, a sheet of white paper, and a pencil. Tell them that they are going to turn an ordinary soft drink can into a symbol of God. Explain the following process in your own words:

Fold the paper so that it fits around the can up to the top and bottom edge.

Mark with a pencil where the paper meets itself, so that you know how much surface you have to use.

Write the words "God can" in big, bold letters on the available area of the paper.

Make a variety of markers and other craft supplies available. Invite the young people to decorate the surface of the wrapper any way they want to. Encourage them to be creative and cover the surface entirely. The can represents God's concern over their worries.

3. When the young people are finished decorating their wrapper, have them tape it to the can. If you have time, have them share their cans with one another.

4. Give everyone a few small pieces of paper. Tell them to think about what it is that they need to give over to God, who is quite willing to hold on to the worries for them. Encourage them to be as honest as they possibly can because no one will see their concerns but them. When they are ready, they should write their concerns on a piece of paper and put them in the God can.

Encourage them to take their God can home, keep it in their room, and add to it whenever they are feeling anxious and overwhelmed. Each time they add a concern to the can, they should take a deep breath and say to themselves, "I give this over to you, God. Be with me today."

ALTERNATIVE APPROACHES

◎ Instead of wrapping the can in regular paper, use white contact paper. It will last longer.

◎ Follow the activity with a prayer service during which the young people hear words of comfort in times of struggle. Include a blessing of the God cans.

SCRIPTURAL CONNECTIONS

◎ Matt. 6:25–34
◎ Matt. 11:28–30
◎ Matt. 14:22–32

NOTES

Use the space below to jot notes and reminders for the next time you use this strategy.

Appendix 1

Connections to the Discovering Program by HELP Strategy

"Build Your Star: A Reflection Exercise on Identity"

This strategy may be used with any course in the Discovering Program, especially the following three:
- ◎ *Dealing with Tough Times*
- ◎ *Growing Up Sexually*
- ◎ *Understanding Myself*

"Life in a Bag: An Introduction Activity"

This strategy may be used with any course in the Discovering Program, especially the following three:
- ◎ *Becoming Friends*
- ◎ *Learning to Communicate*
- ◎ *Understanding Myself*

"Being Michelangelo: An Exercise in Perspectives"

As presented, this strategy complements the following Discovering courses:
- *Becoming Friends*
- *Dealing with Tough Times*
- *Learning to Communicate*
- *Making Decisions*
- *Understanding Myself*

"Pass the Bag: A Biblical Affirmation Exercise"

This strategy may be used with any course in the Discovering Program, especially the following four:
- *Becoming Friends*
- *Exploring the Bible*
- *Learning to Communicate*
- *Understanding Myself*

"Wander and Ponder: A Reflection and Dialogue Activity"

This strategy may be used with any course in the Discovering Program, especially the following five:
- *Being Catholic*
- *Learning to Communicate*
- *Making Decisions*
- *Meeting Jesus*
- *Praying*

"You Can Do It! A Learning Activity on Endurance"

As presented, this strategy complements the following Discovering courses:
- *Dealing with Tough Times*
- *Exploring the Story of Israel*
- *Making Decisions*
- *Understanding Myself*

"Soaring Spirits: An Affirmation Project"

This strategy may be used with any course in the Discovering Program, especially the following five:
- *Becoming Friends*
- *Dealing with Tough Times*

- *Meeting Jesus*
- *Praying*
- *Understanding Myself*

"The Light of Christ: A Candleholder-Making Activity"

This strategy may be used with any course in the Discovering Program, especially the following five:
- *Being Catholic*
- *Celebrating the Eucharist*
- *Gathering to Celebrate*
- *Meeting Jesus*
- *Praying*

"Excuses, Excuses: A Drama and Discussion Activity"

As presented, this strategy complements the following Discovering courses:
- *Being Catholic*
- *Celebrating the Eucharist*
- *Gathering to Celebrate*

"Feelings Charades: A Communication Activity"

This strategy may be used with any course in the Discovering Program, especially the following five:
- *Becoming Friends*
- *Dealing with Tough Times*
- *Growing Up Sexually*
- *Learning to Communicate*
- *Understanding Myself*

"If I Were Candy: A Self-Disclosure Activity"

This strategy may be used with any course in the Discovering Program, especially the following four:
- *Becoming Friends*
- *Learning to Communicate*
- *Making Decisions*
- *Understanding Myself*

"In Sync: A Lesson in Group Dynamics"

This strategy may be used with any course in the Discovering Program, especially the following four:

- ⊚ *Becoming Friends*
- ⊚ *Being Catholic*
- ⊚ *Gathering to Celebrate*
- ⊚ *Learning to Communicate*

"Here I Am!
A Self-Disclosure and Affirmation Activity"

As presented, this strategy complements the following Discovering courses:

- ⊚ *Becoming Friends*
- ⊚ *Learning to Communicate*
- ⊚ *Making Decisions*
- ⊚ *Understanding Myself*

"Take Me Out to the Ball Game:
A Reflection and Discussion Exercise"

As presented, this strategy complements the following Discovering courses:

- ⊚ *Being Catholic*
- ⊚ *Celebrating the Eucharist*

"Church Search: Church Tour and Vocabulary Lesson"

As presented, this strategy complements the following Discovering courses:

- ⊚ *Being Catholic*
- ⊚ *Celebrating the Eucharist*
- ⊚ *Gathering to Celebrate*

"The Journeys of Jesus: A Lesson on Biblical Travels"

As presented, this strategy complements the following Discovering courses:

- ⊚ *Exploring the Bible*
- ⊚ *Meeting Jesus*

"Line It Up: A Timeline Learning Activity"

As presented, this strategy complements the following Discovering courses:

- ⊚ *Being Catholic*
- ⊚ *Exploring the Bible*

◎ *Exploring the Story of Israel*
◎ *Meeting Jesus*

"KGOD Eyewitness News Nazareth: A Television Interview Simulation"

As presented, this strategy complements the following Discovering courses:
◎ *Being Catholic*
◎ *Celebrating the Eucharist*
◎ *Exploring the Bible*
◎ *Exploring the Story of Israel*
◎ *Meeting Jesus*
◎ *Seeking Justice*

"Know Your Scripture: An Activity to Memorize Scripture Verses"

This strategy may be used with any course in the Discovering Program, especially the following four:
◎ *Exploring the Bible*
◎ *Exploring the Story of Israel*
◎ *Meeting Jesus*
◎ *Praying*

"Spotlight on the Sacraments: Discussion and Presentation"

As presented, this strategy complements the following Discovering courses:
◎ *Being Catholic*
◎ *Gathering to Celebrate*

"Sacraments Mobile: A Craft and Discussion Exercise"

As presented, this strategy complements the following Discovering courses:
◎ *Being Catholic*
◎ *Celebrating the Eucharist*
◎ *Gathering to Celebrate*

"Jackpot! A Review Activity"

As presented, this strategy complements the following Discovering courses:
- Being Catholic
- Celebrating the Eucharist
- Exploring the Bible
- Exploring the Story of Israel
- Gathering to Celebrate
- Growing Up Sexually
- Meeting Jesus
- Seeking Justice

"Snowball Fight: An Icebreaker and Timeline Exercise"

As presented, this strategy complements the following Discovering courses:
- Being Catholic
- Celebrating the Eucharist
- Exploring the Bible
- Exploring the Story of Israel
- Meeting Jesus

"Popcorn: A Review Exercise"

As presented, this strategy complements the following Discovering courses:
- Being Catholic
- Celebrating the Eucharist
- Exploring the Bible
- Exploring the Story of Israel
- Gathering to Celebrate
- Growing Up Sexually
- Meeting Jesus
- Seeking Justice

"What's the Meaning? A Vocabulary Review Exercise"

As presented, this strategy complements the following Discovering courses:
- Being Catholic
- Celebrating the Eucharist
- Exploring the Bible
- Exploring the Story of Israel
- Gathering to Celebrate

- *Growing Up Sexually*
- *Learning to Communicate*
- *Meeting Jesus*
- *Seeking Justice*

"M&M Memory Starters: A Review Exercise"

As presented, this strategy complements the following Discovering courses:
- *Being Catholic*
- *Celebrating the Eucharist*
- *Exploring the Bible*
- *Exploring the Story of Israel*
- *Gathering to Celebrate*
- *Meeting Jesus*
- *Seeking Justice*

"Deal Me In! A Review Activity with Playing Cards"

This strategy may be used with any course in the Discovering Program, especially the following seven:
- *Being Catholic*
- *Celebrating the Eucharist*
- *Exploring the Bible*
- *Exploring the Story of Israel*
- *Gathering to Celebrate*
- *Meeting Jesus*
- *Seeking Justice*

"Sacramental Journey: Pilgrimage, Prayer, and Discussion"

As presented, this strategy complements the following Discovering courses:
- *Being Catholic*
- *Gathering to Celebrate*
- *Praying*

"Doodle Prayers: A Creative Prayer Activity"

This strategy may be used with any course in the Discovering Program, especially the following three:
- *Being Catholic*
- *Meeting Jesus*
- *Praying*

"Prayer Box: Creating a Portable Sacred Space"

This strategy may be used with any course in the Discovering Program, especially the following three:
- *Meeting Jesus*
- *Praying*
- *Understanding Myself*

"Prayer Pillows: A Prayer Craft Project"

This strategy may be used with any course in the Discovering Program, especially the following five:
- *Dealing with Tough Times*
- *Making Decisions*
- *Meeting Jesus*
- *Praying*
- *Understanding Myself*

"Prayer with Empty Pockets: A Spontaneous Prayer Exercise"

This strategy may be used with any course in the Discovering Program, especially the following two:
- *Praying*
- *Understanding Myself*

"Three Questions: An Exercise in Shared Prayer"

This strategy may be used with any course in the Discovering Program, especially the following two:
- *Being Catholic*
- *Praying*

"Communication Golf: A Lesson on Obstacles to Communication"

As presented, this strategy complements the following Discovering courses:
- *Becoming Friends*
- *Learning to Communicate*
- *Understanding Myself*

"Balloon Relay Race:
A Lesson in Community and Perseverance"

This strategy may be used with any course in the Discovering Program, especially the following four:
◎ *Being Catholic*
◎ *Dealing with Tough Times*
◎ *Exploring the Story of Israel*
◎ *Seeking Justice*

"A Gift from Jesus: A Guided Reflection with Clay"

This strategy may be used with any course in the Discovering Program, especially the following four:
◎ *Dealing with Tough Times*
◎ *Making Decisions*
◎ *Meeting Jesus*
◎ *Praying*

"Broken Pots:
A Lesson in Piecing Together a History"

As presented, this strategy complements the following Discovering courses:
◎ *Being Catholic*
◎ *Celebrating the Eucharist*
◎ *Meeting Jesus*
◎ *Praying*
◎ *Understanding Myself*

"God Can: An Exercise in Letting Go"

This strategy may be used with any course in the Discovering Program, especially the following five:
◎ *Dealing with Tough Times*
◎ *Growing Up Sexually*
◎ *Making Decisions*
◎ *Meeting Jesus*
◎ *Praying*

Appendix 2

Connections to the Discovering Program by Discovering Course

Becoming Friends

The following HELP strategies complement this course:
- "Life in a Bag: An Introduction Activity"
- "Being Michelangelo: An Exercise in Perspectives"
- "Pass the Bag: A Biblical Affirmation Exercise"
- "Soaring Spirits: An Affirmation Project"
- "Feelings Charades: A Communication Activity"
- "If I Were Candy: A Self-Disclosure Activity"
- "In Sync: A Lesson in Group Dynamics"
- "Here I Am! A Self-Disclosure and Affirmation Activity"
- "Communication Golf: A Lesson on Obstacles to Communication"

Being Catholic

The following HELP strategies complement this course:
- "Wander and Ponder: A Reflection and Dialogue Activity"
- "The Light of Christ: A Candleholder-Making Activity"
- "Excuses, Excuses: A Drama and Discussion Activity"

- "In Sync: A Lesson in Group Dynamics"
- "Take Me Out to the Ball Game: A Reflection and Discussion Exercise"
- "Church Search: Church Tour and Vocabulary Lesson"
- "Line It Up: A Timeline Learning Activity"
- "KGOD Eyewitness News Nazareth: A Television Interview Simulation"
- "Spotlight on the Sacraments: Discussion and Presentation"
- "Sacraments Mobile: A Craft and Discussion Exercise"
- "Jackpot! A Review Activity"
- "Snowball Fight: An Icebreaker and Timeline Exercise"
- "Popcorn: A Review Exercise"
- "What's the Meaning? A Vocabulary Review Exercise"
- "M&M Memory Starters: A Review Exercise"
- "Deal Me In! A Review Activity with Playing Cards"
- "Sacramental Journey: Pilgrimage, Prayer, and Discussion"
- "Doodle Prayers: A Creative Prayer Activity"
- "Three Questions: An Exercise in Shared Prayer"
- "Balloon Relay Race: A Lesson in Community and Perseverance"
- "Broken Pots: A Lesson in Piecing Together a History"

Celebrating the Eucharist

The following HELP strategies complement this course:
- "The Light of Christ: A Candleholder-Making Activity"
- "Excuses, Excuses: A Drama and Discussion Activity"
- "Take Me Out to the Ball Game: A Reflection and Discussion Exercise"
- "Church Search: Church Tour and Vocabulary Lesson"
- "KGOD Eyewitness News Nazareth: A Television Interview Simulation"
- "Sacraments Mobile: A Craft and Discussion Exercise"
- "Jackpot! A Review Activity"
- "Snowball Fight: An Icebreaker and Timeline Exercise"
- "Popcorn: A Review Exercise"
- "What's the Meaning? A Vocabulary Review Exercise"
- "M&M Memory Starters: A Review Exercise"
- "Deal Me In: A Review Activity with Playing Cards"
- "Broken Pots: A Lesson in Piecing Together a History"

Dealing with Tough Times

The following HELP strategies complement this course:
- "Build Your Star: A Reflection Exercise on Identity"
- "Being Michelangelo: An Exercise in Perspectives"
- "You Can Do It! A Learning Activity on Endurance"
- "Soaring Spirits: An Affirmation Project"

- "Feelings Charades: A Communication Activity"
- "Prayer Pillows: A Prayer Craft Project"
- "Balloon Relay Race: A Lesson in Community and Perseverance"
- "A Gift from Jesus: A Guided Reflection with Clay"
- "God Can: An Exercise in Letting Go"

Exploring the Bible

The following HELP strategies complement this course:
- "Pass the Bag: A Biblical Affirmation Exercise"
- "The Journeys of Jesus: A Lesson on Biblical Travels"
- "Line It Up: A Timeline Learning Activity"
- "KGOD Eyewitness News Nazareth: A Television Interview Simulation"
- "Know Your Scripture: An Activity to Memorize Scripture Verses"
- "Jackpot! A Review Activity"
- "Snowball Fight: An Icebreaker and Timeline Exercise"
- "Popcorn: A Review Exercise"
- "What's the Meaning? A Vocabulary Review Exercise"
- "M&M Memory Starters: A Review Exercise"
- "Deal Me In! A Review Activity with Playing Cards"

Exploring the Story of Israel

The following HELP strategies complement this course:
- "You Can Do It! A Learning Activity on Endurance"
- "Line It Up: A Timeline Learning Activity"
- "KGOD Eyewitness News Nazareth: A Television Interview Simulation"
- "Know Your Scripture: An Activity to Memorize Scripture Verses"
- "Jackpot! A Review Activity"
- "Snowball Fight: An Icebreaker and Timeline Exercise"
- "Popcorn: A Review Exercise"
- "What's the Meaning? A Vocabulary Review Exercise"
- "M&M Memory Starters: A Review Exercise"
- "Deal Me In! A Review Activity with Playing Cards"
- "Balloon Relay Race: A Lesson in Community and Perseverance"

Gathering to Celebrate

The following HELP strategies complement this course:
- "The Light of Christ: A Candleholder-Making Activity"
- "Excuses, Excuses: A Drama and Discussion Activity"
- "In Sync: A Lesson in Group Dynamics"

- "Church Search: Church Tour and Vocabulary Lesson"
- "Spotlight on the Sacraments: Discussion and Presentation"
- "Sacraments Mobile: A Craft and Discussion Exercise"
- "Jackpot! A Review Activity"
- "Popcorn: A Review Exercise"
- "What's the Meaning? A Vocabulary Review Exercise"
- "M&M Memory Starters: A Review Exercise"
- "Deal Me In! A Review Activity with Playing Cards"
- "Sacramental Journey: Pilgrimage, Prayer, and Discussion"

Growing Up Sexually

The following HELP strategies complement this course:
- "Build Your Star: A Reflection Exercise on Identity"
- "Feelings Charades: A Communication Activity"
- "Jackpot! A Review Activity"
- "Popcorn: A Review Exercise"
- "What's the Meaning? A Vocabulary Review Exercise"
- "God Can: An Exercise in Letting Go"

Learning to Communicate

The following HELP strategies complement this course:
- "Life in a Bag: An Introduction Activity"
- "Being Michelangelo: An Exercise in Perspectives"
- "Pass the Bag: A Biblical Affirmation Exercise"
- "Wander and Ponder: A Reflection and Dialogue Activity"
- "Feelings Charades: A Communication Activity"
- "If I Were Candy: A Self-Disclosure Activity"
- "In Sync: A Lesson in Group Dynamics"
- "Here I Am! A Self-Disclosure and Affirmation Activity"
- "What's the Meaning? A Vocabulary Review Exercise"
- "Communication Golf: A Lesson on Obstacles to Communication"

Making Decisions

The following HELP strategies complement this course:
- "Being Michelangelo: An Exercise in Perspectives"
- "Wander and Ponder: A Reflection and Dialogue Activity"
- "You Can Do It! A Learning Activity on Endurance"
- "If I Were Candy: A Self-Disclosure Activity"
- "Here I Am! A Self-Disclosure and Affirmation Activity"

◎ "Prayer Pillows: A Prayer Craft Project"
◎ "A Gift from Jesus: A Guided Reflection with Clay"
◎ "God Can: An Exercise in Letting Go"

Meeting Jesus

The following HELP strategies complement this course:
◎ "Wander and Ponder: A Reflection and Dialogue Activity"
◎ "Soaring Spirits: An Affirmation Project"
◎ "The Light of Christ: A Candleholder-Making Activity"
◎ "The Journeys of Jesus: A Lesson on Biblical Travels"
◎ "Line It Up: A Timeline Learning Activity"
◎ "KGOD Eyewitness News Nazareth: A Television Interview Simulation"
◎ "Know Your Scripture: An Activity to Memorize Scripture Verses"
◎ "Jackpot! A Review Activity"
◎ "Snowball Fight: An Icebreaker and Timeline Exercise"
◎ "Popcorn: A Review Exercise"
◎ "What's the Meaning? A Vocabulary Review Exercise"
◎ "M&M Memory Starters: A Review Exercise"
◎ "Deal Me In! A Review Activity with Playing Cards"
◎ "Doodle Prayers: A Creative Prayer Activity"
◎ "Prayer Box: Creating a Portable Sacred Space"
◎ "Prayer Pillows: A Prayer Craft Project"
◎ "A Gift from Jesus: A Guided Reflection with Clay"
◎ "Broken Pots: A Lesson in Piecing Together a History"
◎ "God Can: An Exercise in Letting Go"

Praying

The following HELP strategies complement this course:
◎ "Wander and Ponder: A Reflection and Dialogue Activity"
◎ "Soaring Spirits: An Affirmation Project"
◎ "The Light of Christ: A Candleholder-Making Activity"
◎ "Know Your Scripture: An Activity to Memorize Scripture Verses"
◎ "Sacramental Journey: Pilgrimage, Prayer, and Discussion"
◎ "Doodle Prayers: A Creative Prayer Activity"
◎ "Prayer Box: Creating a Portable Sacred Space"
◎ "Prayer Pillows: A Prayer Craft Project"
◎ "Prayer with Empty Pockets: A Spontaneous Prayer Exercise"
◎ "Three Questions: An Exercise in Shared Prayer"
◎ "A Gift from Jesus: A Guided Reflection with Clay"
◎ "Broken Pots: A Lesson in Piecing Together a History"
◎ "God Can: An Exercise in Letting Go"

Seeking Justice

The following HELP strategies complement this course:

◎ "KGOD Eyewitness News Nazareth: A Television Interview Simulation"
◎ "Jackpot! A Review Activity"
◎ "Popcorn: A Review Exercise"
◎ "What's the Meaning? A Vocabulary Review Exercise"
◎ "M&M Memory Starters: A Review Exercise"
◎ "Deal Me In! A Review Activity with Playing Cards"
◎ "Balloon Relay Race: A Lesson in Community and Perseverance"

Understanding Myself

The following HELP strategies complement this course:

◎ "Build Your Star: A Reflection Exercise on Identity"
◎ "Life in a Bag: An Introduction Activity"
◎ "Being Michelangelo: An Exercise in Perspectives"
◎ "Pass the Bag: A Biblical Affirmation Exercise"
◎ "You Can Do It! A Learning Activity on Endurance"
◎ "Soaring Spirits: An Affirmation Project"
◎ "Feelings Charades: A Communication Activity"
◎ "If I Were Candy: A Self-Disclosure Activity"
◎ "Here I Am! A Self-Disclosure and Affirmation Activity"
◎ "Prayer Box: Creating a Portable Sacred Space"
◎ "Prayer Pillows: A Prayer Craft Project"
◎ "Prayer with Empty Pockets: A Spontaneous Prayer Exercise"
◎ "Communication Golf: A Lesson on Obstacles to Communication"
◎ "Broken Pots: A Lesson in Piecing Together a History"